The Up & Running Series from SYBEX

■ ■ ■ ■ ■ ■ ■ ■ ■

Other titles include Up & Running with:

- AutoSketch 3
- Carbon Copy Plus
- DOS 3.3
- DR DOS 5.0
- Flight Simulator
- Grammatik IV 2.0
- Harvard Graphics
- Lotus 1-2-3 Release 2.2
- Lotus 1-2-3 Release 2.3
- Lotus 1-2-3 Release 3.1
- Norton Utilities
- Norton Utilities 5
- Norton Utilities on the Macintosh
- PageMaker 4 on the PC
- PageMaker on the Macintosh

- PC Tools Deluxe 6
- PC-Write
- PROCOMM PLUS
- Q & A
- Quattro Pro 3
- Quicken 4
- ToolBook for Windows
- Turbo Pascal 5.5
- Windows 3.0
- Windows 286/386
- WordPerfect 5.1
- WordPerfect Library/ Office PC
- XTreeGold 2
- Your Hard Disk

Computer users are not all alike.
Neither are SYBEX books.

We know our customers have a variety of needs. They've told us so. And because we've listened, we've developed several distinct types of books to meet the needs of each of our customers. What are you looking for in computer help?

If you're looking for the basics, try the **ABC's** series, or for a more visual approach, select **Teach Yourself.**

Mastering and **Understanding** titles offer you a step-by-step introduction, plus an in-depth examination of intermediate-level features, to use as you progress.

Our **Up & Running** series is designed for computer-literate consumers who want a no-nonsense overview of new programs. Just 20 basic lessons, and you're on your way.

SYBEX **Encyclopedias** provide a comprehensive reference and explanation of all of the commands, features and functions of the subject software.

Sometimes a subject requires a special treatment that our standard series doesn't provide. So you'll find we have titles like **Advanced Techniques, Handbooks, Tips & Tricks,** and others that are specifically tailored to satisfy a unique need.

You'll find SYBEX publishes a variety of books on every popular software package. Looking for computer help? Help Yourself to SYBEX.

For a complete catalog of our publications:

SYBEX Inc.
2021 Challenger Drive, Alameda, CA 94501
Tel: (415) 523-8233/(800) 227-2346 Telex: 336311
Fax: (415) 523-2373

Up & Running with
Word for Windows™

. . . .

Bob Campbell

SYBEX®

San Francisco ■ Paris ■ Düsseldorf ■ Soest

Acquisitions Editor: Dianne King
Series Editor: Joanne Cuthbertson
Editor: Richard Mills
Technical Reviewer: Sheldon Dunn
Word Processors: Deborah Maizels, Scott Campbell, and Susan Trybull
Series Designers: Ingrid Owen and Helen Bruno
Icon Designer: Helen Bruno
Technical Art: Delia Brown
Screen Graphics: Cuong Le
Desktop Production Artist: Suzanne Albertson
Proofreader: Patsy Owens
Indexer: Julie Kawabata
Cover Designer: Archer Design

SYBEX Up & Running Books

■ ■ ■ ■ ■ ■ ■ ■ ■

The Up & Running series of books from SYBEX has been developed for committed, eager PC users who would like to become familiar with a wide variety of programs and operations as quickly as possible. We assume that you are comfortable with your PC and that you know the basic functions of word processing, spreadsheets, and database management. With this background, Up & Running books will show you in 20 steps what particular products can do and how to use them.

Who this book is for

Up & Running books are designed to save you time and money. First, you can avoid purchase mistakes by previewing products before you buy them—exploring their features, strengths, and limitations. Second, once you decide to purchase a product, you can learn its basics quickly by following the 20 steps—even if you are a beginner.

What this book provides

The first step usually covers software installation in relation to hardware requirements. You'll learn whether the program can operate with your available hardware as well as various methods for starting the program. The second step often introduces the program's user interface. The remaining 18 steps demonstrate the program's basic functions, using examples and short descriptions.

Contents & structure

A clock shows the amount of time you can expect to spend at your computer for each step. Naturally, you'll need much less time if you only read through the step rather than complete it at your computer.

Special symbols and notes

You can also focus on particular points by scanning the short notes in the margins and locating the sections you are most interested in.

In addition, three symbols highlight particular sections of text:

The Action symbol highlights important steps that you will carry out.

The Tip symbol indicates a practical hint or special technique.

The Warning symbol alerts you to a potential problem and suggestions for avoiding it.

We have structured the Up & Running books so that the busy user spends little time studying documentation and is not burdened with unnecessary text. An Up & Running book cannot, of course, replace a lengthier book that contains advanced applications. However, you will get the information you need to put the program to practical use and to learn its basic functions in the shortest possible time.

We welcome your comments SYBEX is very interested in your reactions to the Up & Running series. Your opinions and suggestions will help all of our readers, including yourself. Please send your comments to: SYBEX Editorial Department, 2021 Challenger Drive, Alameda, CA 94501.

Preface

■ ■ ■ ■ ■ ■ ■ ■ ■

Microsoft Word for Windows offers you a level of power and flexibility without equal among word processors. For instance, you have an unequalled wealth of possibilities for defining the appearance of your documents, incorporating graphic images and tables, and circulating a document for comments or revisions. What is more, these and other features are well integrated into the program, accessible, and easy to learn. Although Word for Windows is rich in features and sometimes offers a choice of means to the same end, once you begin working with the program (with a little guidance), you will find its organization makes any given task simple and intuitive.

Up and Running with Word for Windows is designed as a systematic tutorial introduction to the program, for users with at least a little experience with PCs or word processing. For this reason, if at all possible, do work through this book from beginning to end with the program up and running, and carry out the simple exercises to the letter. They are designed to familiarize you with Word's features quickly, with a minimum of typing. Further tips throughout will help you to generalize from the examples to any methods you need apply in your work.

Your practice will put the book's examples in concrete, immediate relation to the actions of your hands and the program's behavior on-screen. If you try things out, operations that appear complex will quickly become second nature. Pay special attention to steps 2, 3, and 4, which will teach you the basics of interacting with Word for Windows.

Bob Campbell
April 1991

Table of Contents

Installation

The Setup program provided with Word for Windows makes installation very straightforward. Because Word files are stored on the distribution disks in compressed form, and because Setup must take note of your hardware, you must use this program to install Word for Windows.

SYSTEM REQUIREMENTS

To run Word for Windows, you need a PC with at least an 80286 processor, 1MB of memory, a hard disk with at least 3.2MB of available space (4.2MB to include the useful tutorial), a floppy-disk drive, and a video system compatible with EGA, VGA, or other standards supported by Windows itself. You must have Microsoft Windows 2.11 or later or Windows/386 installed on your system.

To realize the fullest performance from this large and powerful program, you should have a 20MHz or faster 80386 processor and abundant memory. Because Word for Windows reads from and writes to the disk intensively, it is helpful to have 1 to 2MB of extended memory available to devote to a disk cache (such as SMARTDrive, supplied with Windows). Optimal operation may thus require 4MB or more of total memory.

USING THE SETUP PROGRAM

Backing up your disks

As when installing any new software, before you do anything else, make backup copies of your distribution disks and put the originals away for safekeeping. Use the DISKCOPY command in DOS to copy each of the four disks (your package may have three) in the format that you will use (3½-inch or 5¼-inch). Label each copy: **Setup, Conversions, Utilities,** and **Learning/Writing Aids.** Use these copies for the actual installation described next.

Starting Setup

You can run the Setup program from Windows. From the Program Manager, choose File Run. (Use your mouse to click on File in the menu bar and click on Run in the menu that appears, or, alternatively, press Alt-F and then R on your keyboard. Alternate forms of commands are described in Step 2.) Insert your Setup disk in drive A, and enter **a:setup** in the Command Line text box (use any available floppy drive).

Here's how to use Setup: Highlight a selection (when multiple selections are offered) using the Up Arrow and Down Arrow keys, and then press Enter to continue. Where it is possible to select more than one item, highlight each choice and press Enter (it will be marked with an asterisk). Finally, highlight the topmost choice, Continue With Selected *Items,* and press Enter to continue. If you need to cancel the installation at any time, press Ctrl-X.

Read the opening screen and press Enter. Press Enter at the following screen, with the choice *Install Word for Windows and utilities* highlighted. Press Enter after reading the note that appears.

Select a hard-disk drive letter with the arrow keys and press Enter. (Use a drive with adequate space, preferably the one containing your Windows files.) Press Enter once again to accept the program directory name offered, *D:\WINWORD*, and wait while Setup copies some files.

When prompted, insert the Conversions disk, press Enter, and wait again while files are copied. If you expect to use Word for Windows to edit documents produced by other word processors, highlight *Install conversions* and press Enter now. (Otherwise, select *Do not install conversions.*) When you select a conversion, Word for Windows can recognize the corresponding document type and convert it to or from its own format. Highlight each conversion that you want and press Enter. (Note that you must scroll down from the top for each selection.) When you have done this—or if you don't want any conversions—select the topmost item, Continue With Selected Conversions, and press Enter once more. Allow Setup to copy more files.

Conversions

Just as conversions allow you to read documents produced by other word processors, *graphics filters* allow you to incorporate graphics produced by other programs in your Word for Windows documents. You can install filters to convert, for instance, Lotus .PIC files or PC Paintbrush .PCX files. Highlight your choices and continue as you did when choosing conversions. Allow time for copying.

Graphics filters

If you have adequate disk space, select *Install tutorial lessons* and press Enter. When prompted, insert the Utilities disk and press Enter. When prompted again, insert the Learning/Writing Aids disk and press Enter.

The tutorial

At this point, you can install drivers for certain printers not supported by Windows. These printers, mostly daisy-wheel printers, are listed in the back of your *Printer Guide,* under "Unsupported

Printer drivers

Printers." To install any of them, select *Install Word for DOS printer drivers* now. Select your printer type or types and continue as you did for conversions.

PCL soft fonts If you will be printing on an HP LaserJet or compatible printer, which accepts fonts designed for Hewlett-Packard's Printer Control Language, select *Do install symbol soft fonts* now, and follow the prompts. When prompted, reinsert the Setup disk. Word for Windows is now installed on your hard disk.

ADDING WORD TO WINDOWS

Setup leaves it to you to add Word for Windows to an existing program group.

1. Select <u>W</u>indow from the menu bar in the Program Manager.

2. Select a group for Word (such as Main).

3. Select <u>F</u>ile <u>N</u>ew, click the Program Item button if it is not selected, and click OK.

4. Type the description **Word for Windows**.

5. Press Tab to reach the Command Line text box.

6. Type in *D:*\winword\winword.exe, using your drive letter for *D*, and click OK. The Word for Windows icon appears, indicating that the program is ready to run.

CREATING A PRACTICE DIRECTORY

Before ending this session, create a directory to hold your practice files for this book. You can call this directory *D:\PRACTICE*. Create the directory in DOS or by using the Windows File Manager (double-click on the File Manager icon in the Program Manager's Main window, click on the icon of the drive you want, select File Create Directory, and enter the new directory path).

Face to Face
with Word

Becoming acquainted with Word for Windows is a small instance of "learning how to learn"—the Windows environment places all the program's resources in front of you, and you only need to discover how to use them.

STARTING WORD FOR WINDOWS

To start the program, double-click on the Word for Windows icon in the Program Manager's Main window. The first time that you run Word for Windows, a dialog box appears prompting you for your name and initials. Notice the vertical bar, called the *insertion point*, to the left of the Name box. Type in your name; as you do so, your initials appear automatically in the box below. Click the OK command button (the oblong area on the right) or press Enter to continue.

THE PROGRAM AND DOCUMENT WINDOWS

Word for Windows now displays the screen shown in Figure 2.1, ready for you to enter text. The basic screen elements are labeled in the figure. The *title bar* across the top of the screen shows the name of the program, Microsoft Word, and a working title for your first document, Document1.

Divide the screen into a *program window* and a *document window* by selecting <u>W</u>indow <u>A</u>rrange All. In this form, the document is

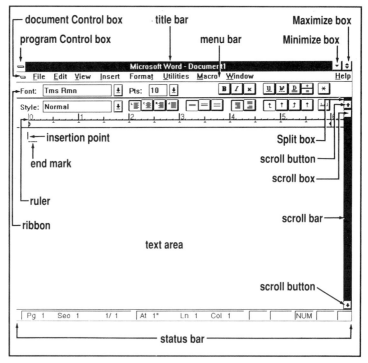

■ *Figure 2.1: The document window*

given its own title bar. Each window has a *Control box* to the left of the title bar; the Control box for the program controls the program window as a whole, and the box for the document controls just that document window. Try clicking on the Control box for the document window. If you were now to select Close, you would close the new document. Selecting Close from the Control box for Microsoft Word, on the other hand, would end this program session. For now, press Esc to close the menu.

Each window also has a *Minimize box* (the downward-pointing triangle) and a *Maximize box* (the upward-pointing triangle or the pair of triangles) in its upper-right corner. Click on the Maximize box in the document window to merge the two windows again. In the merged form, the program and document names appear together in one title bar, as they did when you began the program. You will find that the merged form is handy for working on a single document; the separated form allows you to view several documents at once.

USING MENUS

The *menu bar,* located under the program title bar, accepts commands in several forms. Consider this example: Word offers alternative *views,* or ways of displaying documents. For instance, normal document view, which you see when the program first starts up, conveys document formatting information accurately, while draft view is the most convenient form for high readability and rapid text entry. You will learn more about views in Step 17, but for now, try each of these methods of toggling draft view, that is, of turning it on and off:

- Using the mouse, click on View in the menu bar, then click on Draft in the submenu.

- Using the keyboard, press and release Alt and then press V

Alternative ways of accessing commands

to open the View menu. (You always select a menu item by pressing the underscored letter, which is not necessarily the first letter.) Note that a check mark appears beside Draft, indicating that draft mode is on. Press D to turn it off.

- Press V while pressing and holding Alt. This more conventional key combination is useful if, for instance, you are running Windows under the program DESQview, which uses Alt as its hot key.

- Press F10 to activate the menu bar. Press the Right Arrow key three times to highlight View, and press Enter to select it. Press Down Arrow to highlight Draft and press Enter to select it. At this point, draft view should be off.

You can combine these forms—for instance, you can press Alt-V, move to Draft with Down Arrow, and press Enter. Throughout this book, something like "select View Draft" will be used to describe sequences like these.

Word for Windows offers both short and long menus. The long, or full, menus display more possible choices. This book assumes that you have full menus visible. Select View now. If the lowest item is Full Menus, select it to make these menus available. If it is Short Menus, cancel the choice by clicking on View or pressing Esc. Full menus should now be visible. Note that "ghosted" menu items (such as Footnotes and Annotations under View) are not currently available.

DIALOG BOXES

When submenu items require you to enter text or to make choices among alternatives, they lead to dialog boxes. This is true of all submenu items ending with an ellipsis (...).

Select Utilities Customize to bring up a dialog box, as shown in Figure 2.2. This box shows most of the features of a typical dialog box, which you can recognize by their shapes:

- Command buttons

- Option buttons

- Check boxes

- Text boxes

You can select one of these features in any of three ways:

- Using your mouse, click on a button or check box, or within a text box. This will select an option button

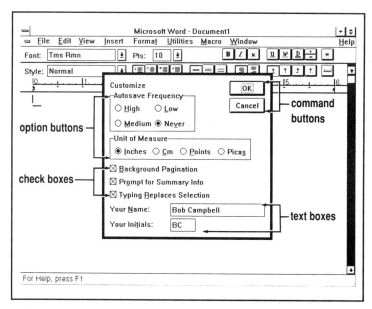

- *Figure 2.2: A typical dialog box*

(which blackens), toggle the value of a check box (adding or removing an *X*), or place an insertion point (a vertical bar marking where you can insert or delete text, using the keyboard and the Del or Backspace key) in a text box.

■ Press Tab or Shift-Tab until the box or cluster of buttons you want to change is marked by a dotted box. You can then use the arrow keys to choose a button from a group, use the spacebar to toggle the value of a check box, or type a new value into a text box. If a selection in a text box is marked (it appears in reverse video), you need only begin typing to replace it.

■ Type the underscored letter corresponding to the button or box to select it, to toggle its value, or to enter text. Note that some command buttons have no corresponding letter.

When text in a dialog box is highlighted, to select another option, you must press Alt and the letter, not just the letter by itself.

Try these methods now to modify settings for option buttons and check boxes in this window. When you are finished, select Cancel to prevent making permanent changes to these settings.

SPECIAL SCREEN ELEMENTS

This section introduces three special screen elements of Word for Windows: the *ribbon,* the *ruler,* and the *status bar.*

Ribbon   You can see the ribbon immediately below the menu bar in Figure 2.1. The ribbon provides a quick way to format characters (setting the font, point size, and emphasis). You will learn more about ribbon in Step 11. In the meantime, you can remove it from the screen by selecting View Ribbon to delete its check mark.

Ruler   The ruler, which appears just below the ribbon, provides a quick way to set paragraph style (alignment, spacing, and tabs). It is also covered in Step 11. You can remove it from the screen for now by selecting View Ruler.

The status bar appears at the bottom of the screen. It displays the following information: *Status bar*

- The left third shows the current page number as it will be printed, the current section number (see Step 8), and the number of pages you are from the beginning of the document, along with the page total.

- The middle third shows the distance of the current line from the top edge of the current page, the line number on the current page, and the current column number. The first two values do not appear in draft mode.

- The right third displays indicators of macro recording in progress, multiple-column mode, Typeover mode (see Step 3), and other specialized information, as well as Caps Lock and Num Lock indicators.

THE KEYBOARD TEMPLATE

You can perform many operations in Word for Windows directly from the keyboard. All valid keystroke actions are shown on the keyboard template supplied with the program. Observe that keypad and function-key commands are color-coded according to the Shift-key legend printed near the middle of the template. For instance, under *Home, Beginning of Line* appears in red, indicating that you can return the insertion point to the beginning of the current line by pressing Home alone; *Beginning of Doc* appears in brown, indicating that you can move to the beginning of the current document by pressing Ctrl-Home.

WORKING WITH THE TEXT AREA

The *text area* is the central screen region, devoted to text entry and editing. Figure 2.1 shows its basic elements: The vertical *insertion point* shows where text that you type will be entered, the *end mark* signifies the end of the document, and the *mouse pointer* (in its I-beam form) allows you to move the insertion point by positioning and clicking.

The vertical *scroll bar* is also associated with this region. It allows you to scroll through the document—slowly, by putting the mouse pointer on one of the *scroll buttons* (marked with an up or down arrow) and holding down the left mouse button, or rapidly, by putting the pointer on the *scroll box* that lies between the buttons and dragging it. The dark oblong just above the upper scroll button is the *Split box,* which you can drag down the scroll bar to divide the window into two *panes,* as described in Step 13. You will learn more about elements of the text area in Step 3.

USING HELP

Word for Windows offers a comprehensive help system that works both as a reference guide and as context-sensitive help for any situation. Bring up the Help menu by selecting Help. From here, you can select a general index, topics pertaining to the keyboard, or topics pertaining to the active window and the current view. Press F1 to get context-sensitive help from any menu. Pressing this key from the text area brings up the Help index.

Within a Help window, you will find phrases with a solid underline—these are known as *jump terms,* because you can jump to a further explanation of one by clicking on it (with the mouse pointer, transformed into a pointing hand) or by highlighting it using the arrow keys and pressing Enter. You can then return to the previous screen by selecting Browse Backtrack or by pressing F9.

You will also find phrases with a broken underline—these are known as *defined terms*. Click on them or highlight them and press Enter to see a definition, which will disappear when you release the mouse button or key. You can search through a list of terms by typing the first letter of the topic you want.

Select Help Tutorial for a set of useful tutorials on Word for Windows topics.

To end your first Word for Windows session, just select Close from the program window Control box. Since you have made no changes to the document, you return directly to the Program Manager.

Ending your session

Creating a Document

In this step, you will learn the basic skills of creating a document, entering text, moving the insertion point, and saving a document.

STARTING A NEW DOCUMENT

Start Word for Windows by clicking on its icon in the Program Manager window. This will open the default document, Document1, as before, but it is more flexible to begin a new document.

Select File New. The dialog box shown in Figure 3.1 appears. Note that the insertion point is located in the Use Template text box, which is accompanied by a list box. Templates, which you will learn how to use and create in Step 19, are a means of preserving format information for a class of documents. You can scroll through the list box to highlight a template, or you can enter the name of a template in the text box. For now, however, leave the default template, NORMAL, highlighted.

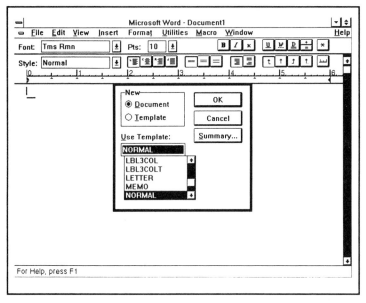

- *Figure 3.1: The new file dialog box*

Select Summary to bring up the summary information dialog box,
shown in Figure 3.2. Note that your document now has the new
temporary name Document2. It still exists only in the computer's
memory, so the directory name field is blank.

Note these additional features of the dialog box:

- The document's title. This will appear in the document
  window's title bar.

- The document's subject. You can type in a description up to
  255 characters long.

- The document's author. This is initially the name you gave
  when you first started the program, but you can change it.

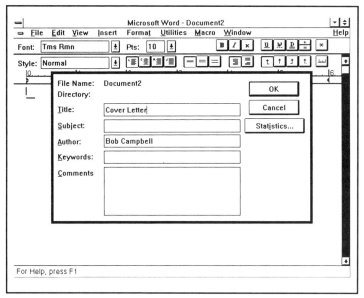

■ *Figure 3.2: The summary information dialog box*

- ■ Keywords. You can type in a series of words separated by spaces that describe the document. You can later use one or more of these words to search for the document on disk.

- ■ Comments. You can type in up to 255 characters of further remarks about the document.

All these items can also be incorporated into the document's text through the use of *fields,* which are inserted in a document to be replaced by preset or calculated values at print time. You will see one simple example of a field below, and several more in the course of this book.

For now, just type **Cover Letter** in the Title box, where the insertion point is already located.

The Statistics command button leads to another dialog box listing facts about the current document. Try selecting it now. After perusing the contents, select OK to close the statistics box, and then select OK one more time to close the summary information box itself. This act returns you to the text area, with the insertion point in the upper-left corner of the screen, ready to accept text.

ENTERING TEXT

Paragraphs   Understand the basic idea of a *paragraph* in Word for Windows. A carriage return and any preceding text form a paragraph, which can be formatted as a unit. Even a single line, such as a title, can form a paragraph.

Your first exercise in entering text will be composing a short letter. To make matters simple, it will be block style, with all contents flush-left. For your line breaks to follow those in the example, choose draft view, if necessary, by selecting <u>V</u>iew <u>D</u>raft.

Begin the document by typing in today's date. Then, press Enter twice to make the date a paragraph followed by a blank line.

The paragraph is one of the basic units of document formatting. Sometimes you want to treat a block of text as a paragraph while keeping each element on a line of its own. Enter the following two lines of an inside address. To make them the same paragraph, press Shift-Enter instead of Enter alone after the first line. Press Enter twice after the second line.

```
12359 Industrial Loop
Alameda, CA 94501
```

Then, type this inside address, remembering to separate the lines by pressing Shift-Enter:

```
Dr. Onorio Vasquez, Director
Costabel Wildlife Refuge
Box 1
Costabel, FL 32789
```

Enter the salutation, then press Enter twice:

```
Dear Dr. Vasquez:
```

Next, type the body of the letter. This time, allow word wrap by typing continuously without pressing Enter until the end. Type the misspelled words as they appear:

```
As you can see from my enclosed resume, my
extensive experience as a COBOL programer and
systems analist demostrates the planning
ability and attention to detail erquired of a
Dune Restoration Intern at your institution.
May I please have an interview at your
convenience? I look forward to relocating to
Florida.
```

You can make newlines (the characters produced by pressing Shift-Enter) and end-of-paragraph marks visible on-screen by selecting View Preferences Paragraph Marks so that the check box is marked. Before selecting OK, consider the other view options available in this dialog box. For instance, you can make spaces or tabs visible characters on-screen.

Press Enter twice, type **Sincerely**, and press Enter twice again. Now, try adding a field. Select Insert Field, highlight Author in the list box, and select OK. Your name should appear at the bottom of the letter.

You can switch between viewing a field code (Author) and its value (your name). Select Ⅴiew Field Ⅽodes so that this menu item is check-marked, and the code will appear. Select it again, and the value of the field will replace it.

INSERTING AND OVERWRITING TEXT

To see how Insert mode works, move the mouse pointer so that it falls between the *m* and the *e* in *programer,* click to move the insertion point there, and type the missing *m*. Then, to try Typeover mode, press Ctrl-Right Arrow to reach the word *analist,* and press Right Arrow alone to place the insertion point to the left of the letter *i*. Press Ins so that OVR appears in the status line, and type y to type over the *i*. Press Ins again to return to Insert mode. Leave *demonstrates* as it is until you learn how to use the spelling checker in Step 6. For now, press Down Arrow and Home to reach the start of the next line, press Del twice, and type **re** to repair *required*. Note that Del deletes the character to the right of the insertion point, and Backspace deletes the character to the left.

When you use the mouse to move the insertion point to the left margin, don't click with the pointer so far to the left that the pointer becomes an arrow pointing up and right. You are then in a special area called the *selection bar,* where clicking has a different effect. (The selection bar is described in Step 4.)

Dividing and uniting paragraphs

Experiment with dividing one paragraph into two:

1. Set Ⅴiew Prⅇferences Ⅽpaces and Ⅽaragraph Marks for a more graphic view of what you are doing.

2. Place the insertion point to the left of the *M* in *May I please....*

3. Press Enter twice to create a new paragraph preceded by a blank line.

4. Press Backspace twice to shrink the text back to one paragraph. You can edit paragraph endings just as you do ordinary text.

Select Help Keyboard and click on the subheading *Moving the insertion point within text* under Movement Keys (or highlight the heading and press Enter). After viewing the contents, take a few minutes to try out some of the keystrokes listed here for navigating the text section. They are also listed on the right side of your keyboard template.

SAVING A NEW DOCUMENT

To save your document, select File Save As. Type the path name **d:\practice\cover** in the Save File Name text box, but use the drive letter and directory name you chose at the end of Step 1. Word for Windows will add its default document extension, .doc, to the file name. You can now exit Word for Windows as you did in Step 2.

You can select File Save As to name a document at any time after creating it, not only just before you exit the program.

Working with Blocks of Text

In this step, you will learn the basics of selecting a block of text and performing an operation on that block, such as deleting it, copying it, or replacing it.

As you edit text with Word for Windows, you use a principle called "select, then do." First you select some text (or a picture, or part of a table), and then you perform some operation on it. In the previous step, you selected new text by placing the insertion point. The text was entered in the current format. In this step, you will select existing text by highlighting it.

OPENING A DOCUMENT

Select File. The last file that you edited, COVER.DOC, appears toward the bottom of the submenu as choice 1. (Up to the last four edited files will appear.) You need only press 1 to bring it up, but wait before doing so.

Instead of selecting the file here, select Open, type **d:\practice** (or your path name) in the Open File Name text box, and press Enter. Double-click on the name COVER.DOC in the list box—the file will be ready to edit. At this point, it should look like Figure 4.1 (shown in draft view). Now you know how to bring up a file that you may not have edited recently.

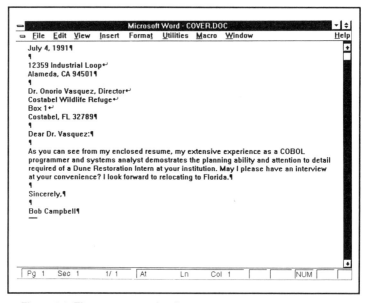

- *Figure 4.1: The current practice document*

SELECTING TEXT

You can select text by using the mouse or any of a variety of keyboard commands. Using the mouse is the simplest way to select an arbitrary block of text.

Selecting Text with the Mouse

Try using the mouse to select different areas:

1. Align the mouse pointer just at the left edge of the *I* in *Intern* in the letter body.

2. Press and hold the left mouse button. Without releasing the button, sweep the mouse first right and then left. Note the extent of the highlighting.

3. Return to the starting point and sweep the mouse directly down one line.

4. Release the button and move the mouse to one side.

Deselecting Text

You must learn how to remove highlighting before proceeding any further. This, too, can be done with the mouse or from the keyboard:

■   Click the left mouse button; the highlighting disappears. Note that the insertion point moves to the current mouse pointer line.

■   Alternatively, just press an arrow key. Try this method after marking some fresh text.

Using the Selection Bar

The selection bar is an area at the left edge of the screen, beyond the left margin. You can use it to select a line, a paragraph, or the entire document.

1. Position the mouse pointer to the left of a line of the inside address so that it becomes an arrow pointing up and right.

2. Click the mouse to select a line. (This includes the line ending.)

3. Deselect the line by pressing any arrow key.

4. Double-click with the mouse to select the entire address.

5. Deselect the line again, and click while depressing the Ctrl key to select the whole letter.

6. Deselect the line once more.

Selecting Text from the Keyboard

To select text from the keyboard, follow these steps:

1. Move the insertion point to the left edge of the *D* in *Dune*.

2. Highlight the word *Dune* (and the following space) by pressing Shift-Ctrl-Right Arrow.

3. Press the Right Arrow key to clear the marking, and press Shift-Ctrl-Right Arrow again. You can inch through the text word for word by repeating this combination.

4. Now, do it in reverse, pressing Shift-Ctrl-Left Arrow first and then Left Arrow alone.

If your separate arrow keys do not work properly, try using the arrow keys on your numeric keypad, with Num Lock turned off.

Select Help Keyboard and click on the jump term *Selecting text* under Selection Keys. Try some of the key combinations listed there, which also appear on the right side of your keyboard template.

Extending a Selection

After you have highlighted text, you can turn on the Extend feature. Then, more text that you want to select is added to the highlighted area.

1. Select the first line of the body of the letter by clicking with the mouse in the selection bar.

2. Press F8 to turn on the Extend feature.

3. Press Ctrl-Right Arrow to extend the selection a few words. (Any command to move the insertion point will add to the selection.)

4. Press Esc to turn off the Extend feature, and then press any arrow key to turn off the highlighting.

Marking an Oblong Area

Instead of marking text line by line, you can mark an oblong box.

1. Move the insertion point just to the left of the *D* in *Dr.* in the inside address by clicking there.

2. Press Shift-Ctrl-F8 to turn on column selection.

3. Move the mouse cursor to the salutation line, below and to the right of the *r* in *Director.*

4. Click the mouse. The entire inside address will be highlighted. Try clicking at other points to see how the box dimensions change.

5. Press Esc to turn off column selection.

You can delete, copy, or move the marked area. If you delete an oblong area within a running paragraph, surrounding text shifts to fill in the void.

You can also highlight an oblong dynamically, without choosing columns mode, simply by dragging with the right mouse button depressed. Try this as well.

DELETING AND REPLACING TEXT

Nothing could be simpler than deleting or replacing marked text.

1. Place the mouse pointer anywhere on the word *extensive* in the body of the letter and double-click to mark it.

2. Press Del. The word is gone.

3. Mark the word *relocating* in the same way.

4. Type **moving**—it will automatically replace the marked text.

5. You can undo a change of this sort by pressing Alt-Backspace—try it.

For this automatic replacement to work, the Typing Replaces Selection check box in the Utilities Customize dialog box must be marked.

If, with text highlighted, you unintentionally replace the text by pressing a key other than Esc or an arrow key, immediately press Alt-Backspace to undo the replacement.

CUTTING AND PASTING TEXT

Deleting text moves the text into a local buffer, but cutting text moves it to the Windows Clipboard, from which you can transfer it elsewhere in the same document, to a different document, or even to a different application. As usual, you can select Cut and Paste from either the keyboard or a menu.

1. Mark the phrase *systems analyst* plus the following space by moving the insertion point to the left of the phrase and pressing Shift-Ctrl-Right Arrow twice.

2. Select Edit Cut.

3. Move the insertion point to the left of the *C* in *COBOL* and select Edit Paste.

4. Double-click on the *and* that precedes *demostrates* and press Shift-Del.

5. Position the insertion point before the *C* in *COBOL* again and press Shift-Ins.

Note that copying (select Edit Copy or press Ctrl-Ins) works just as cutting does, except that the original text remains in place.

Copying text

You can paste the last cut or copied text repeatedly, moving the insertion point between paste operations if necessary.

MOVING TEXT

Like deleting, moving is a more direct form of text surgery than cutting and pasting.

1. Select the final sentence, *I look forward to relocating to Florida.* (Don't highlight the paragraph mark.)

2. Press F2, the Move key. The status bar now reads, "Move to where?"

3. Place the insertion point to the left of the *M* in *May I have...* and press Enter.

4. Add the needed space to the end of the moved sentence.

SAVING AN EXISTING FILE

To save the sample text, select File Save or press Shift-F12. Use Shift-Alt-F2 if you don't have an F12 key. Even if you fail to select Save, Word for Windows prompts you to save a changed file as you exit the program.

Make a habit of saving your file whenever you think of it, such as whenever you go for coffee or before you make a global revision. In this way, you protect your work from the effects of power failures or major mistakes.

Now that you have practiced marking paragraphs, hide paragraph marks again by selecting View Preferences and clearing Paragraph Marks. Exit Word for Windows.

Searching and Replacing

■ ■ ■ ■ ■ ■ ■ ■ ■ ■ ■

This step guides you through the essentials of searching for and replacing existing text.

To begin, bring up your practice letter, COVER.DOC, as you did in Step 4.

SEARCHING

Searches are simple to do, but some possibilities may not be obvious; for instance, you can search for ranges of text using wildcards, and you can search for special characters, such as paragraph endings.

Searching for Text

To bring up the Search dialog box (shown in Figure 5.1), just select <u>E</u>dit <u>S</u>earch. Type the text string **to** in the <u>S</u>earch For text box and press Enter. Note that the *to* embedded in *Director* is highlighted.

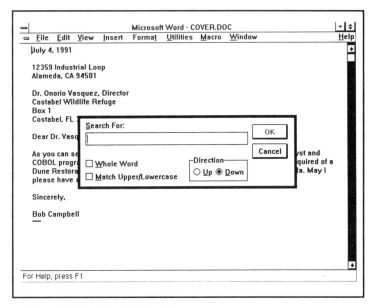

■ *Figure 5.1: The Search dialog box*

Press Ctrl-Home to return the insertion point to the top of the document, and select Edit Search again. This time, check the Whole
Word check box and press Enter. The search will pick out the first
occurrence of the word *to* in the text.

The simplest way to repeat a search is to use the keystroke command. Press Shift-F4 twice more to find the next two occurrences
of the word *to*. Press Shift-F4 again and a dialog box will report
no more occurrences. If you select Yes now, Word for Windows
will begin the search again at the start of the document. Select No
to cancel the search.

There are two other useful options in the Search dialog box.

Check the Match Upper/Lowercase box if you want to find only words exactly matching what you type in case. (For instance, if you search for *cobol* or *Cobol*, you will not match *COBOL*.)

Select the Up option button if you want your search to proceed from the insertion point toward the start of the document. You can search from the bottom of the document upward by pressing Ctrl-End and then checking this option as you search.

Word for Windows uses ? as a wildcard to stand for any single character. Move to the top of the document and search for *m?y*, with the Match check box off. You will see the word *May* highlighted. To search for an actual question mark, include ^? (caret and question mark) in the search string.

You can also search for special characters in a document. Move once again to the top of the document, and search for the string ^p (caret and *p*) to find the first paragraph mark in the letter. Press Shift-F4 to locate the ends of subsequent paragraphs. This method works whether or not paragraph marks are visible.

Bring up the appropriate help section to see a complete list of search keys for special characters:

1. Select Help Index.

2. Select the successive jump terms *Procedures* and *Editing and proofreading*.

3. Press S to reach the first jump term under the Searching heading.

4. Select the next term, *searching: for text*. After you quit Help, try searching the letter for occurrences of the newline character.

Searching for Formatting

Word for Windows allows you to search for formatting in your document. To demonstrate this feature, here is a quick preview of character formatting:

1. Select the phrase *Dune Restoration Intern* in the letter.

2. Press Ctrl-B.

3. Deselect the phrase. It is now formatted in boldface, as you can see in normal editing view.

4. Move the insertion point to the top of the document.

5. Select Edit Search.

6. Press Ctrl-B, type **Dune**, and click OK. The search will lead to the beginning of the phrase in boldface. When you begin your next search, you can turn off the bold emphasis by pressing Ctrl-B again.

To see a list of formats you can search for, refer to the Help item *searching: for formatting*, which precedes *searching: for text*, under the further jump terms *character formatting keys*, *paragraph alignment keys*, and *line-spacing keys*.

REPLACING

You begin a simple replacement much as you do a simple search, except that replacements proceed forward only (of course, you must enter a replacement term).

1. Move to the top of the document.

2. Select Edit Replace.

3. Enter **Dr.** in the Search For box.

4. Press Tab.

5. Enter **Doctor** in the Replace With box.

6. Select OK.

At each occurrence of *Dr.*, Word for Windows will prompt you to make the replacement (Yes), to skip the current instance (No), or to abandon the operation (Cancel). Select Yes in both instances. The operation will terminate automatically after the last instance.

To make a series of replacements without being prompted, select the Confirm Changes check box in the Replace dialog box to remove the check mark. You can also switch to automatic replacement after any given replacement by selecting Confirm in the dialog box.

When you are finished, save the sample document.

Proofing Your Work

This step introduces you to Word for Windows' built-in spelling checker and thesaurus.

To begin, start the program and open your current practice document, LETTER.DOC.

CHECKING YOUR SPELLING

To check spelling throughout a document, start with the insertion point at the beginning and select Utilities Spelling. This brings up the dialog box shown in Figure 6.1. You could begin the check by selecting Start, but this time select Options first.

You can check the spelling of a single word as you edit by highlighting that word, selecting Utilities Spelling, and then selecting Check. If Word for Windows finds a misspelled word, the Spelling dialog box described below appears.

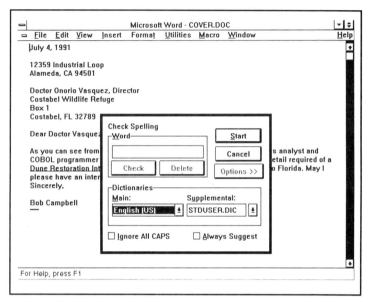

- *Figure 6.1: The Check Spelling dialog box*

Word for Windows uses a main dictionary and a supplemental dictionary. You can create a supplemental dictionary to assemble a specialized lexicon to suit your own needs. Over time, in fact, you can create and add to several supplemental dictionaries, each tailored to one aspect of your work, simply by adding words Word for Windows doesn't recognize to a dictionary.

Select Supplemental and type **practice.dic** in the text box. Now, words that you add during this practice section won't clutter up your default dictionaries. You can select this or another supplemental dictionary in a later session by clicking on the down arrow to the left of this text box to activate its associated list box.

Before continuing, note the two check boxes below. Ignore All CAPS, when checked, instructs the spell-checker not to check any words spelled in all capital letters. Check it if you don't want to be stopped at every obscure acronym in your document during a spell-check. Always Suggest tells the spell-checker to offer a substitute for any word it doesn't recognize, without your prompting it to do so.

When you have entered the dictionary name, select Start. Select Yes in the dialog box to create the supplemental dictionary. At this point, the subsequent Spelling dialog box appears.

Ignoring a word

Sometimes an unrecognized word will be correct, but you will see no need to save it for future use. The first word found in the letter, *Onorio*, is highlighted in the text and is shown under *Not in Dictionary*. Select Ignore to bypass further instances in this document. Bypass *Vasquez* in the same way.

Recording a word

The next suspect word is *Costabel*. Let's suppose that you want this word to be recognized in future sessions. Select Add. The word is added to the supplemental dictionary. Further instances will be bypassed.

Correcting a word

The next word is *demostrates*, which gives you the opportunity to see more features of the spell-checker. Note that the insertion point appears initially in the Change To text box. You will often immediately recognize a typographical error like this and find it easiest to type in a correction and to select Change to make the change. In this case, however, select Suggest to give the spell-checker a chance to guess the correct word. Figure 6.2 shows the Spelling dialog box as it now appears.

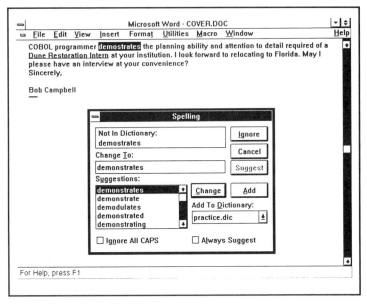

■ *Figure 6.2: The Spelling dialog box*

The spell-checker's guesses appear in the Su̲ggestions list box. All you have to do is scroll to the right word (if necessary) and double-click on it, or highlight it and select C̲hange. If the right word does not appear, you can select the Change T̲o box by pressing Alt-T, enter the correct word, and select C̲hange. For this example, since *demonstrates* is already highlighted, just select C̲hange to make the replacement. Select I̲gnore after each subsequent word until you reach the end of the letter.

CHOOSING YOUR WORDS

A thesaurus leads you to synonyms of a word, allowing you to exercise your judgment to choose the best word for a given context.

A good electronic thesaurus, such as the one incorporated in Word for Windows, makes it very simple and convenient to explore possible synonyms for a word and to make a replacement.

Highlight *demonstrates* in the letter and select Utilities Thesaurus. The Thesaurus dialog box appears, as shown in Figure 6.3. Take a moment to study the elements of the box. They follow a roughly clockwise sequence:

- Look Up text box: initially shows the word that you selected from the text.

- Definitions list box: shows the parts of speech and meanings that the thesaurus knows for the lookup word. Because

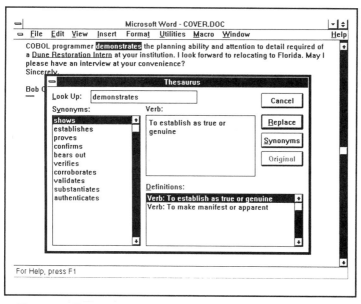

- *Figure 6.3: The Thesaurus dialog box*

meanings may extend beyond the edge of the box, the currently highlighted part of speech and meaning appear in full in the square above the list box.

■ Synonyms list box: shows available synonyms for the currently selected definition of the lookup word. Note that Word for Windows has already pluralized or conjugated them for you to match the lookup word.

Summary of
thesaurus
use

To use the thesaurus, first select the appropriate Definition, and then select the most promising Synonym. If you are satisfied with it, select the command button Replace. If you want to pursue a line of thought further, select Synonym instead and repeat the sequence. To return to the original choice, select Original.

Try this example to find a useful synonym for *demonstrates*:

1. Accepting the initial definition, *Verb: To establish as true or genuine*, and the initial synonym, *shows*, select the command button Synonym.

2. The selected synonym, *shows*, becomes the new lookup word, with its own set of definitions and synonyms.

3. Select Definitions for *shows*, scroll down, and select *Verb: To make manifest or apparent*. (Note that these paths are often more or less circular.)

4. Select Synonyms, highlight *evinces*, and select Replace. The dialog box will be removed, and the word *demonstrates* will be replaced.

If you had found no promising synonyms on this path, you could have selected Original and tried another path.

With your corrections and changes made, save the document.

Simple Printing

■ ■ ■ ■ ■ ■ ■ ■ ■ ■ ■

Printing with Word for Windows is simple, once your printer is set up.

SETTING UP YOUR PRINTER

Before you can print from Word for Windows, your printer must be properly configured under Windows itself. You can review this installation process in a few simple steps:

1. From the Program Manager, select the Control Panel and then Printers in the Control Panel window.

2. If your printer does not appear as an installed printer, select Add Printer and highlight your printer (or a printer that it emulates) in the List of Printers list box. Select Install and insert the requested printer driver disk when prompted.

3. Select Configure and highlight the port to which your printer is connected. Select OK.

4. Make sure that your printer's Status is set to Active and select OK.

Setup from the Control Panel

To set up your printer from Word,

1. Start Word for Windows and open COVER.DOC.

2. Select File Printer Setup.

3. Select your printer from the Printer list box (if it is not already highlighted).

4. From here, select Setup to explore setup options for your printer. The window that appears next assumes different forms for different printers, depending on the features available.

Figure 7.1 shows the setup window for an HP LaserJet III printer, which offers a wealth of options. Most printers will allow you to

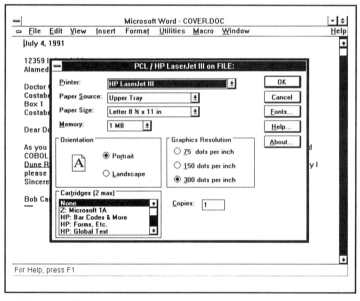

■ *Figure 7.1: Setup for a LaserJet printer*

select Portrait or Landscape orientation. Note that, for the Laser-Jet, you can also enable one or two printer cartridges, install soft fonts after selecting the Fonts command button, set resolution for the printer, and indicate the amount of memory installed in your printer. Note also the Help command button. You can call up a sophisticated help system to answer your questions about LaserJet, PostScript, and some other printers.

Make setup choices for your printer, and select OK in both dialog boxes. Select File once again, and make sure that the Print option is available (it should not be "ghosted").

PRINTING A DOCUMENT

With the practice letter in the current window, follow these steps to print your document:

1. Select File Print to display the Print dialog box shown in Figure 7.2. Note that the box displays the currently selected printer and a few simple options.

2. Type the number of copies you want in the Copies text box, or leave it set for one copy.

3. Select Print All pages, if necessary. You could enter a page number to print from and a page number to print to. Of course, setting a range does not make sense if you have a one-page document. Further options reached by selecting the Options command button are covered in Step 17.

4. Select OK to actually begin printing.

THE PRINT MANAGER

The Print Manager in Windows collects documents to be printed from Windows applications, organizes them into a queue, and

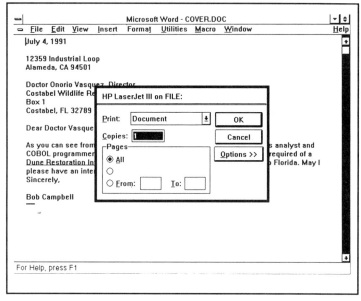

- *Figure 7.2: The Print dialog box*

feeds them to the printer one by one. If the Print Manager has problems, it will display a message box.

Dealing with printer problems

The Print Manager is sensitive to unexpected behavior from a printer or a parallel port. For instance, if your printer goes momentarily offline between printing jobs, you may see an error message, such as "The Print Manager cannot write to LPT1."

If you see such a message, try this:

1. After clearing the message box, minimize Word for Windows (click on the Minimize box near the upper-right corner).

2. Double-click on the Print Manager icon in the Program Manager.

3. Select the Resume command button. Select Resume once or twice more, if necessary, in response to further messages.

You may be able to prevent printer problems by disabling the Print Manager and sending documents directly to the printer. However, you will then no longer be able to put several documents in the queue or to do other work while a document is being printed.

Disabling the Print Manager

To turn off the Print Manager, follow these steps:

1. Bring up the Control Panel from the Program Manager.

2. Double-click on the Printers icon.

3. Clear the Use Print Manager check box.

4. Select OK.

When the document is printed, the Print dialog box will be removed. You can then exit Word for Windows.

Ending the print session

Document Formatting

All that you do to control a document's appearance makes up that document's formatting. Word for Windows organizes formatting into several levels, from the whole document down to individual characters.

As you design documents, you should always follow the same sequence of steps:

- Set formatting for the whole document, which includes page dimensions and margin settings (covered in this step).

- If necessary, define sections and set their formatting (covered in this step). A section is the basic unit for line numbering and multiple columns.

- Make up a paragraph format (Step 9). Paragraph formatting includes indentation, which is defined in terms of dimensions of the whole document.

- Set up character formatting, which includes fonts and point sizes (Step 10).

This step includes a sample document that will give you a chance to try out these techniques.

FORMATTING A WHOLE DOCUMENT

Look at Figure 8.1, which shows the dimensions of a document. Most basic are the *page width* and *page height,* the physical dimensions of the paper used to print the document. There are four areas that comprise the boundaries of the text: the *top* and *bottom*

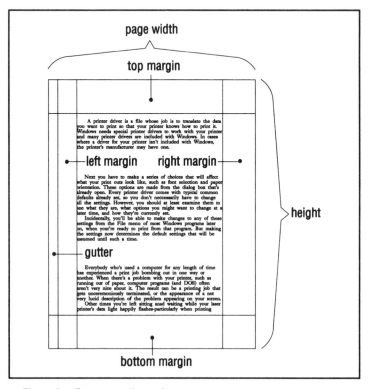

- *Figure 8.1: Document dimensions*

margins and the *left* and *right* margins. You can also add a *gutter* margin to the left margin to allow room to bind the document.

If you were putting together a book with facing pages, the right-hand, or odd-numbered, pages would follow the dimensions in the figure. However, it would make sense to call the left margin the inside margin because of its proximity to the binding, and the right margin the outside margin because of its position. The left-hand pages would then look like a mirror image of the right-hand ones.

Start Word for Windows and, with Document1 in the window, select Format Document to bring up the dialog box shown in Figure 8.2. Note the settings for page width and height. These settings for your printer paper must match the Paper Size setting under Setup

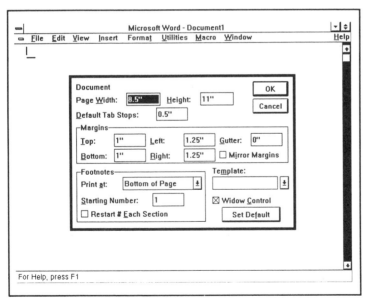

- *Figure 8.2: The Format Document dialog box*

in the Printer Setup dialog box. The default tab stops are spaced at half-inch intervals across the document; this distance can be changed here, but you can also place tabs as part of paragraph formatting.

Try making a small change in the margin settings:

1. Select Left margin, and type **1"** in the text box.

2. Do the same for Right margin.

3. Select Gutter, and set the value to **0.5"** to allow for binding.

You need not type the inch mark, since inches are the default measure for margin widths (as they are for column widths and indents).

Momentarily set Mirror Margins and note that the left and right margins are redefined as inside and outside margins. Select the box again to clear this feature.

Open the *Footnotes Print at* list box to see the options for placement of notes. (Footnote options are described in Step 15.)

Note the Widow Control check box. When set, it keeps page breaks from dividing single lines from the rest of paragraphs. Accordingly, by setting this box, you prevent both *widows* and *orphans*. A widow is the first line of a multiline paragraph at the bottom of a page, and an orphan is the last line of a multiline paragraph at the top of a page.

The remaining features in the dialog box pertain to use of templates to preserve document formatting, which you will read about in Step 19.

FORMATTING SECTIONS

Now is a good time to learn about section formatting, although you will not need it for the practice document.

Creating a Section

Select Insert Break to see how to define the beginning of a section. With the insertion point at the beginning of a paragraph, you can then select Continuous to allow the section to begin on the current page, or you can select one of the page choices to force it to begin on a new page. The section will end where you next repeat this sequence at the beginning of a later paragraph. Select Cancel when you have seen enough of this dialog box.

Formatting a Section

Select Format Section to bring up the dialog box shown in Figure 8.3. Note these features of the box:

You can create multiple columns simply by typing a number greater than one in the Columns Number text box. Text will then snake from one column to the next as you edit it. You can set the spacing between columns in the Spacing text box, and you can draw a vertical rule between columns by setting Line Between. When you leave the dialog box, the new column width takes effect immediately. You can actually *see* the multiple columns as you work by selecting View Page from the program window.

Multiple columns

If you select Footnotes Print at End of Section under Format Document, setting Include Footnotes here causes accumulated footnotes to be printed at the end of the current section; otherwise, they are printed at the end of a later section.

Footnote placement

The Section Start list box allows you to override your Insert Break selection to dictate whether your section begins on a new page.

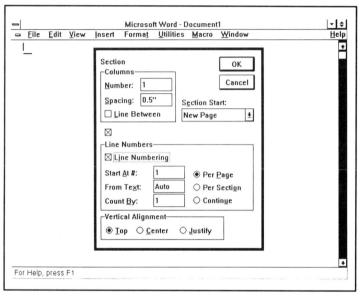

- *Figure 8.3: The Format Section dialog box*

Numbering lines

If you set Line Numbering, lines in the current section will be numbered when printed. The options in the Line Numbers group then become available. Viewed from top to bottom, the text boxes allow you to set a starting line number, to set a distance between the line numbers and the left margin of the text proper, and to print a number for every *n*th line. (A value of 1 tells Word to show a number for every line.) The option buttons control when to start renumbering: on each new page, at each new section, or not at the beginning of this section.

Paragraph alignment

The Vertical Alignment buttons determine how paragraphs are distributed vertically across a page when you print: aligned at the top, aligned at the center, or justified (distributed with equal spacing between the top and bottom margins). There must be extra vertical space available for these options to have any effect.

You can clear the dialog box by selecting Cancel.

ENTERING A NEW PRACTICE DOCUMENT

You will use the practice document shown in Figure 8.4 to explore features of Word for Windows described through Step 18 of this book, so reproduce it carefully. Enter the document, typing each block of text as a continuous paragraph.

Save your document as *D:\PRACTICE\SEASIDE*. Enter the title *Plants of the Pacific Shoreline* for your document when prompted.

Plants of the Central Pacific Shoreline

Plants of the Salt Marshes

Cordgrass (Spartina foliosa)

A widespread plant of the transition zone between marine and terrestrial environments, cordgrass has special adaptations such as salt glands to excrete excess salinity. It is important habitat for an endangered shorebird, the clapper rail.

Pickleweed (Salicornia virginica)

Pickleweed is a widespread plant of middle marsh elevations and vital salt marsh harvest mouse habitat.

Plants of the Dunes

European Beach Grass (Ammophila arenaria)

A hardy colonist, European beach grass was introduced in the early 1900s to stabilize dune formation. It has covered large areas of dunes, displaced many native species, and interfered with natural dune formation, thus contributing to erosion and loss of dune habitat.

American Dune Grass (Elymis mollus)

American dune grass, a rye grass, colonizes dunes less aggressively than European beach grass and is important in efforts to restore native vegetation.

Yellow Sand Verbena (Abronia latifolia)

Yellow sand verbena is another hardy dune colonizer that forms conspicuous mounds. It displays heads of yellow trumpet-shaped flowers from May through August.

■ *Figure 8.4: The practice document*

Formatting Paragraphs

In this step, you will practice the third level of formatting a document—paragraph formatting.

To begin, start Word for Windows and open SEASIDE.DOC, the sample document that you created in the previous step.

SETTING PARAGRAPH INDENTS

To choose a paragraph for formatting, you need only place the insertion point within the paragraph. (Alternatively, you could mark one or more paragraphs.) Place the insertion point anywhere within the first narrative paragraph, which begins, "A widespread plant of the transition zone...." Select Format Paragraph to bring up the dialog box shown in Figure 9.1.

The From Left and From Right indents are measured from the left and right document margins: A positive indent moves the paragraph toward the center of the page; a negative indent moves it

Indent measures

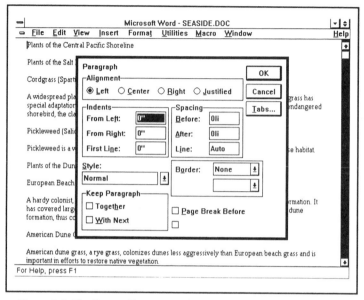

■ *Figure 9.1: The Format Paragraph dialog box*

beyond the margins toward the page edge. A block quotation is a typical use for a positive indent.

As an experiment, give the paragraph a block indent: Set the From Left and From Right text boxes each to 0.5", and select OK to view the effects. Then, bring up the Paragraph dialog box again.

The First Line indent is measured from the left paragraph indent. Restore the From Left and From Right settings to 0", and set First Line to 0.25", Select OK to restore the paragraph to its original width, with a normal paragraph indent.

If you specify a first line of −0.25", you create a hanging indent, where the first line begins to the left of the following lines.

ALIGNING PARAGRAPHS

Paragraph alignment refers to how text is positioned relative to the left and right indents: Left-aligned text is flush-left and ragged-right; right-aligned text is flush-right and ragged-left. Center alignment centers each line of the paragraph between the indents. Justified alignment spreads text between the indents by adding increments of spacing between words.

Justify the paragraph by bringing up the Paragraph dialog box, selecting Justified, and clicking OK. Next, highlight the title paragraph, "Plants of the Central Pacific Shoreline," and select Center from the dialog box. Keep the box on-screen for a moment.

Borders

You can focus attention on a paragraph by drawing a line above it, below it, to its left, or completely around it (as a box). Draw a shadow box around the title: Select Border and highlight Box in the list box, and then select Pattern and highlight Shadow. Click OK.

Spacing

The spacing options allow you to add vertical spaces before, after, or within a paragraph. The default measure is *lines*; for instance, you can double-space a whole document by selecting it (click the mouse while pressing Ctrl with the pointer in the selection bar), bringing up the Paragraph dialog box, selecting Line, and entering *2li* or just *2*.

The default value of Auto for line spacing essentially sets single spacing according to the tallest character in a given line. If you specify *1li*, the effect is the same, except that the paragraph's default font (set by its *style*, described in Step 12) sets a minimum height. You can also specify absolute spacing by entering a negative number. In this case, letters bigger than the default font will be allowed to print overlapping the previous line.

Here's an example of how you can add spacing around paragraphs to make text entry easier and more flexible: For Step 8, as you entered sample text, you probably pressed Enter twice between paragraphs to add a space between them. Have Word for Windows add the space for you, instead.

To strip extra line endings, follow these steps from the text area:

1. Press Ctrl-Home and select Edit Replace.

2. Type ^p^p (representing two line endings) in the Search For box and ^p alone in the Replace With box.

3. Clear Confirm Changes.

4. Press Enter.

Then, to add automatic spacing, follow these steps:

1. Highlight the document by Ctrl-clicking with the mouse from the selection bar.

2. Bring up the Paragraph dialog box again.

3. Select Spacing After.

4. Type in 1li.

5. Press Enter and remove the highlighting.

You can now readily change or remove the added spacing between all paragraphs.

SETTING TABS

Recall that default tab stop intervals are set in the Format Document dialog box. You can set custom tabs as part of paragraph formatting by selecting the Tabs command button, which opens the dialog box shown in Figure 9.2. From this box, you enter a tab position, select an alignment and leader for your new tab, and select Set to make the tab stop effective. You repeat this for each new tab stop and then select OK.

A *leader* is a character that extends from the previous tab stop, as you will see. While a custom tab stop is in effect, it cancels any default tabs to its *left*. Custom tabs remain in effect as you add more paragraphs.

For a quick practice exercise, follow these steps:

1. Open a new document.

2. Select Format Paragraph, and then select Tabs.

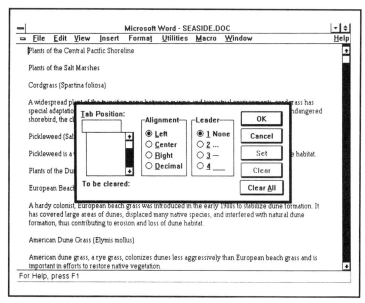

■ *Figure 9.2: The Tabs dialog box*

3. Enter a tab position of **0.5"**.

4. Accept the default alignment and leader, and select <u>S</u>et. The Tab Position text box will be highlighted again.

5. Enter **5"**.

6. Press Alt-D to select <u>D</u>ecimal alignment, press Alt-2 to select a leader of periods, and select <u>S</u>et again.

7. Select OK.

Follow these steps from the text area:

1. Press Tab, type **Land acquisition**, press Tab, type **$75,000.00**, and press Shift-Enter.

2. On the new line, press Tab, type **Hydroseeding**, press Tab, type **$89.75**, and press Enter.

The result is a listing with left-aligned text connected to decimal-aligned figures by periods.

Navigating tabs

Essentially, you edit or navigate across tabs as you do any character. As you saw, to enter a tab character, press Tab. To delete a preceding tab character, press Backspace. You can move across existing tab stops by using the left and right arrow keys. When you have finished experimenting with tabs, save this document as shown, under the name TABSET.DOC for later practice.

You can also bring up the Tabs dialog box from the text area more directly by selecting Forma<u>t</u> <u>T</u>abs. You can highlight any existing tab in the list box and edit it, clear it, or change its options. Text in the current paragraph realigns itself automatically.

Other paragraph formatting

Note the remaining options in the Paragraph dialog box (styles will be covered in Step 12). You can keep Word for Windows from dividing a selected paragraph across pages or separating it from the following paragraph by setting the Keep Paragraph

Together or With Next check boxes. You can force a page break before a paragraph by setting Page Break Before. Finally, if you have set line numbering for the current section, you can suspend it for the current paragraph by clearing Line Numbering.

TRANSFERRING A PARAGRAPH FORMAT

Formatting for a whole paragraph is contained in its paragraph mark.

For the next exercise, select Window and return to the initial document, SEASIDE.DOC. Select View Preferences Paragraph Marks, if necessary, to make the marks visible.

1. Select the paragraph mark that follows *clapper rail* and ends the newly formatted paragraph by placing the selection point to its left and pressing Shift-Right Arrow.

2. Press Shift-F2 to copy the highlighted text.

3. At the "Copy to where?" prompt, move the insertion point to the paragraph mark that ends the next narrative paragraph, after *mouse habitat*.

4. Press Enter. Note that the insertion point and the old paragraph mark have moved to the line below.

5. Press Del to delete the old mark.

Repeat this sequence to reformat the remaining descriptive passages in the text. When you are finished, save the file and exit.

You can join two adjacent paragraphs by selecting the paragraph mark for the first and pressing Del. The first paragraph will take on the format of the second.

Formatting Characters

Character formatting allows you to transform the appearance of characters in your document, whether a single character, a range of characters, or all the characters. For instance, you can change a character's font (from Courier to Times Roman, for example), its size (from 10-point to 14-point), and its emphasis (from roman to boldface or italic).

To begin, open the sample document, SEASIDE.DOC.

CHOOSING FONTS

Highlight the document title, "Plants of the Central Pacific Shoreline," and select Format Character to bring up the dialog box shown in Figure 10.1. The choices that you make here will apply character formatting to highlighted text (as in this case) or to newly entered text. To change the font, select Font and highlight Helvetica or Helv in the list box. Choose another font if neither of these is displayed.

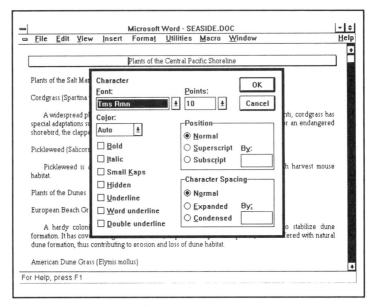

- *Figure 10.1: The Format Character dialog box*

If you highlight characters with different fonts or sizes, no initial values will appear in the corresponding list boxes. You can still apply a new font, size, or emphasis to all the marked characters.

The different fonts and sizes available to you are normally limited to those available for your printer. To work with fonts and sizes that you cannot actually print, select View Preferences and clear the Display as Printed check box.

**Emphasis
check boxes**

Next, select Points and highlight *12* in the list box to enlarge the title to 12-point text.

The check boxes on the left side of the dialog box add emphasis to characters, such as boldface and underlining. Checking the Small

Kaps box, for instance, changes lowercase letters to small capitals. Check this box now to try this emphasis in your document title.

The command buttons on the right side allow you to increase or decrease character spacing for special effects and situations. For the title, select Expanded and leave the default 3pt expansion in the text box. (You can expand text by as much as 14 points or contract it by as much as 1.75 points.)

Spacing
controls

Note that the dialog box also allows you to set the color of characters (if you have a color display or printer) or their position relative to the baseline of text (for example, for a reference number superscript). Select OK to make the formatting changes.

FORMATTING CHARACTERS FROM THE KEYBOARD

You can also do most kinds of character formatting from the ribbon (described in the next step) or directly from the keyboard.

1. Highlight the first subheading, *Plants of the Salt Marshes.*

2. Press Ctrl-F2 to increase the size of the font to the next larger size (12 points).

3. Press Ctrl-I to italicize the title.

4. Press Ctrl-B to boldface the title. You can see the ease with which you can apply more than one emphasis to selected text. Note that these shortcut keystrokes are listed on your keyboard template.

5. Highlight *Cordgrass (Spartina foliosa).*

6. Press Ctrl-I to italicize this title. (Leave the remaining titles to practice using the ribbon in the next step and applying styles in Step 12.)

7. Try applying emphasis to newly entered text: Highlight *It* at the beginning of the sentence that reads, "It is important habitat..." in the next paragraph. Press Ctrl-I and type **Spartina** to replace the word.

CONTROLLING LINE BREAKS

Word for Windows gives you some useful options for controlling where your lines break, automatically or manually.

Hyphenating Automatically

You can have Word for Windows create line breaks to help fill lines. To try this, press Ctrl-Home to return to the top of the sample document, and select U̲tilities H̲yphenate. From the dialog box shown in Figure 10.2, select Y̲es to begin the process. The illustration shows the first word found. Word for Windows will break the word at the highlighted hyphen unless you choose another one with the mouse or arrow keys. Select Y̲es to accept the break, and move on to the next word. When the process is over, press an arrow key to remove highlighting from the document.

If you had cleared the Confirm check box, the program would have made all line breaks at once. The Hot Zone text box is also worth mentioning: Word for Windows will attempt to break a line if there is more than this amount of free space at the end of a ragged line or within a justified line. Thus, if you decrease the hot zone, you will get more even lines, but you will also get lots of hyphens, and vice versa.

Controlling Breaks Manually

You can also manually insert hyphen and space characters to control line breaks.

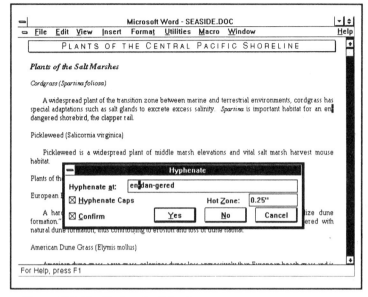

- *Figure 10.2: The Hyphenate dialog box*

Hyphenation
options

- Just type a hyphen, and the program will break a line after it, if necessary.

- Press Ctrl-hyphen to insert a hyphen that will normally appear or print only when it is used to break a line, such as the ones inserted automatically above. If you select View Preferences Show All, these hyphens will appear as angled characters.

- Press Ctrl-Shift-Hyphen to insert a hyphen within text that you don't want broken, such as a telephone number. This character normally looks like a normal hyphen but, with Show All, it looks like an em dash.

Space
character
options

- When you press the spacebar, you enter a space that allows wordwrap. With Show All these spaces look like centered dots.

■ To keep a phrase together on a line, press Ctrl-Shift-space-bar to insert a nonbreaking space. With Show All, these spaces look like degree signs.

OTHER SPECIAL CHARACTERS

The ANSI character set used with Windows contains many characters not found on your keyboard. You can include these characters in your document by using your numeric keypad. You will find a complete table in Appendix C of your *User's Reference*.

Add a pair of open and close double quotation marks to the sample document:

1. Move the insertion point to the beginning of the word *stabilize* in the narrative paragraph under *European Beach Grass*.

2. Press and hold Alt and type *0147* from the keypad.

3. Move the insertion point past the period at the end of the sentence, and press Alt-0148 in the same way. You can now save the sample document.

Common special characters

Here are some other commonly used characters and the keystrokes to produce them:

Single open quote	Alt-0145
Single close quote	Alt-0146
Em dash	Alt-0150
En dash	Alt-0151
One-quarter	Alt-0188
One-half	Alt-0189
Three-quarters	Alt-0190

Quick Formatting

■ ■ ■ ■ ■ ■ ■ ■ ■ ■ ■

You can make the character- and paragraph-formatting options you use most often available on-screen at all times, for more convenient, rapid formatting. The screen elements that include these formatting options are the ribbon and the ruler, respectively.

To begin, bring up SEASIDE.DOC and make these elements visible, as shown in Figure 11.1 (if they are not), by selecting View Ribbon and View Ruler in turn.

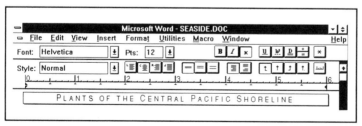

■ *Figure 11.1: The ribbon and the ruler*

USING THE RIBBON

The ribbon offers most of the options available from the Format Character dialog box. You can use the ribbon's font and point-size list boxes much as you do the corresponding options in the dialog box. To reach the font box, for example, click on the down arrow to its right and scroll to and click on the desired font; alternatively, you can press Ctrl-F, open the list box (optionally) by pressing Alt-Down Arrow, bring up the desired font using the up and down arrow keys, and press Enter. The corresponding key combination to reach the point-size box is Ctrl-P.

Ribbon icons
The icons to the right mostly correspond to the emphasis check boxes in the dialog box. From left to right, they are the following:

- Boldface

- Italics

- Small caps

- Continuous underlining

- Underlining by the word

- Double continuous underlining

- Superscripted text (the plus sign above)

- Subscripted text (the equal sign below)

- Special marks (the star). This icon, when set, makes visible any special characters not already selected through View Preferences.

Setting icons
You can set or clear an icon by clicking on it or by pressing the corresponding key combination. Where only one emphasis of a set can be in effect (as for kinds of underlining), you can also clear an icon by setting another icon of the group. When set, an icon appears to be pressed down on a high-resolution monitor or is shown highlighted on a low-resolution monitor. Icon letters will appear to

be ghosted or uncolored when highlighted text contains more than one value for that format quality, but you can still set the icon to apply consistent formatting to all marked text.

Highlight the heading paragraph *Pickleweed (Salicornia virginica)* and click the *I* icon to italicize the phrase.

USING THE RULER

The ruler has three distinct views, *paragraph view*, *margin view*, and *column view*, the last of which is available when you edit a table and will be discussed in Step 18. You rotate between views by clicking on the *ruler-view icon*, the comb-shaped button at the upper right of the ruler. Ruler icons operate like the ribbon icons described above.

Margin View

Click the ruler-view icon to bring up margin view. Note that the ruler is now based on the total page width, rather than the left margin. This view provides a quick way to set margins, otherwise set through the Format Document dialog box.

Note that the current margins are marked by brackets at the bottom of the ruler. The current right margin is at 7¼". Drag the bracket to exactly 7¼", and note the effect on the document formatting. Drag it back to 7¼" to restore the original width.

Paragraph View

Click the ruler-view icon to return to paragraph view. In this view, the ruler provides many of the formatting features found under Format Paragraph. Move the insertion point into the narrative paragraph under *European beach grass* (the one that begins, "A hardy colonist…") to experiment with this paragraph.

Indent markers

Note the three triangular marks below the ruler scale. The mark at the right is the *right-indent marker*. At the left, the upper mark is the *left-indent marker*, and the lower mark is the *first-line marker*. You can change indents for the current paragraph (or for marked paragraphs) by dragging these marks.

Try these simple changes, noting the effect after each:

1. Drag the first-line marker back to 0" to remove the paragraph indent.

2. Drag the left-indent marker to ¼ ". Note that the first-line marker moves with it, giving you a block indent.

3. While depressing and holding the Shift key, drag the left indent back to 0", restoring the original format. With the Shift key depressed, the left-indent marker moves alone.

Paragraph alignment icons

The four icons to the right of the style box set your paragraph to left-aligned, centered, right-aligned, and justified, respectively. Click each of these icons in turn and note the effects. Click the rightmost icon to justify the paragraph again.

Spacing icons

The next three icons set single spacing, one-and-a-half spacing, and double spacing. Try each one. Also try the next two buttons, the second of which inserts a space before the paragraph; the first removes it.

Editing Tabs from the Ruler

Open the practice document that you created in Step 10, TABSET.DOC, for the next experiments.

The four icons to the right of the paragraph-spacing icons set a type for tab stops to be entered. From left to right, they set right-aligned, centered, left-aligned, and decimal tabs. Marks for tab stops appear under the ruler scale: Default tabs appear as inverted Ts, and tabs that you have created are marked like the icons.

Tab icons

Try these simple methods for editing tab stops:

- *Move* a tab stop you have created by dragging its mark to a new position on the scale. Try moving the decimal stop one-half inch to the right by dragging its mark to 5½".

- *Create* a tab stop by clicking the appropriate icon (if it isn't already set), positioning the mouse pointer under the scale, and clicking. Create a new left-aligned tab stop at ½" by clicking on the leftmost tab icon, moving the mouse directly under ½" on the scale, and clicking. Move the insertion point to the beginning of the first line, press Tab, and type **1.** (including the period). Then move to the beginning of the second line, press Tab, and type **100.** (including the period).

- *Delete* a tab stop that you have created by dragging it off the ruler. Try removing your newly created tab stop in this way. Replace this tab stop with a right-aligned one by clicking the third tab icon and clicking again at the half-inch mark.

Exit Word for Windows, confirming that you want to save each practice document.

Global Formatting

■ ■ ■ ■ ■ ■ ■ ■ ■ ■

To control character and paragraph formatting of repeated elements in a document or a class of documents, you should define that formatting using *styles*. This step introduces you to the craft of defining and applying styles.

Open the practice document SEASIDE.DOC to begin.

DEFINING STYLES

The most systematic way to define styles is through the corresponding dialog box. Select Format Define Styles to bring up the box, and select Options to see its fuller form, as shown in Figure 12.1. The list box offers a selection of standard Word for Windows style names. Other standard styles, such as those for headers and footers, appear in the box as you use them. You can also define new styles based on the old ones. Here, you will adapt some of the standard styles to reflect your previous document formatting.

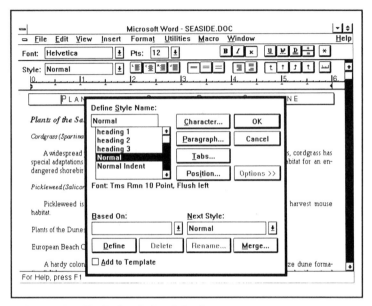

- *Figure 12.1: The Define Styles dialog box*

Normal is your usual default style. To adapt the normal style for this document to your previous settings, highlight Normal in the Define Style Name list box, and select Paragraph to bring up the Paragraph dialog box that you worked with in Step 9. Set the Alignment to Justified, Spacing After to *1li*, and First Line to *.25"*. Click OK.

Note that the Next Style for this style is also Normal. This setting allows you to enter a series of normal paragraphs without reapplying a style.

Heading styles

The heading styles are convenient means for defining different levels of headings; the outlining feature that you will work with in Step 13 uses them in this way.

1. Highlight heading 1 in the list box.

2. Select Yes when prompted to save changes to Normal.

3. Select Character to bring up the familiar Format Character dialog box.

4. From here, set Font to Times Roman or the equivalent.

5. Set the Italic check box, and clear the Underline check box.

6. Press Enter.

7. Select Paragraph, and set Spacing Before to *0li*, Spacing After to *1li*, and First Line back to *0"*.

8. Press Enter.

For heading 1, the Next Style option is also set to Normal, so that, after you enter a heading paragraph, your running text automatically reverts to the Normal style.

Highlight heading 2 in the list box and select Yes. If prompted to change the properties of the standard style, select Yes again. Set paragraph formatting the same as for heading 1; set character formatting the same as for heading 1, except set the point size to 10. Although the original second-level heads were not boldfaced, leave the boldfacing set for a further experiment. Press Enter.

Note the other formatting options. The Tabs command button brings up the Tabs dialog box that you saw in Step 9. The Position command button offers further options for placing the paragraph.

You can easily create a new style for use wherever you choose. You can do this by typing a new style name in the Define Style Name text box, highlighting an existing style in the Based On box (this is optional; the default base style is Normal), and customizing your style as you did above.

The command buttons and check box at the bottom of the box pertain to applying styles across documents, a subject that you will learn more about in Step 19.

APPLYING STYLES

Press Enter (selecting Yes again if prompted) to save your styles and to return to the work area. To apply a style, highlight a paragraph from the selection bar (or just move the insertion point into that paragraph), and select your chosen style from the ruler-style list box. Alternatively, highlight the paragraph, select Format Styles, highlight your chosen style from the list box there, and press Enter. If you are prompted to redefine the style, select No. Try this technique on the sample text:

1. Select the heading paragraph *Plants of the Salt Marshes.*

2. Press Ctrl-S.

3. Open the list box by pressing Alt-Down Arrow.

4. Select *heading 1.* Make sure not to redefine the style.

5. Follow the same procedure with *Plants of the Dunes.*

6. Similarly, apply the heading-2 style to the remaining headings, those with the plant names. The narrative paragraphs are already in the new Normal style and can be left alone.

CHANGING A STYLE BY EXAMPLE

You can change a style globally by example, that is, by editing the new format into a paragraph and incorporating it into the style. As an example, try this:

1. Highlight the heading *European Beach Grass (Ammophila arenaria).*

2. Press Ctrl-B to remove the boldfacing.

3. Press Ctrl-S for styles (the current style, heading 2, will appear in the box), and press Enter.

4. This time, select Yes at the query box to redefine the style.

Boldfacing will disappear from all paragraphs of this style in the document. Where different formats appear in a paragraph, Word for Windows will adopt the formatting of the majority of characters to decide the style.

You can display existing styles on-screen by opening a vertical *Style area* screen region called the *style area*. Select View Preferences, Style Area Width, type in a nonzero value (1" is a useful value), and click OK. A style name will appear to the left of each paragraph. You can close this area by setting the width value to 0" again.

Save your sample document with its styles to end your practice for this step.

DECIDING BETWEEN FORMATTING METHODS

By this time, you have learned several methods for formatting a document. Keep these considerations in mind when deciding among them:

■   Use the ribbon and the ruler to make quick, ad-hoc changes occasionally in a document.

■   Use the dialog boxes to set initial formatting for a block of text in greater detail.

■   Use styles to set formats that you will use repeatedly in the course of a long document.

■   Incorporate your styles in a template (described in Step 19) to make them a standard for a whole class of documents.

Outlining

In this step, you will try your hand at outlining in Word for Windows. Outlining looks a bit esoteric on paper but proves surprisingly easy and intuitive as you begin working with it. It is an invaluable aid in organizing your writing and can also help you browse through long, complex documents. You can also use an outline to number parts of a document or to prepare a table of contents.

The outlining feature makes good use of the mouse, and not all operations are available without one. Accordingly, this step emphasizes mouse operations. Use your previous practice document, SEASIDE.DOC, to work through the exercises.

DISPLAYING AN OUTLINE

Select <u>V</u>iew <u>O</u>utline. The ruler is replaced by the *Outline icon bar,* and the text itself is specially indented. Each paragraph now has its own icon to the left. Outlined plus or minus icons represent headings, and a small square icon represents body text, the lowest outline level. A heading that has further subheadings or body text (together called its *subtext*) is represented by a plus icon, and a heading that has neither is represented by a minus icon. You can see that, at the moment, all headings have subtext.

Expanding or Collapsing a Whole Outline

Look at the icon bar and note the Show icons to the right. By clicking on one of these icons, you determine how many heading levels deep you want to display the outline. The initially selected icon, All, prompts display of all heading levels plus the body text.

 To display only the first lines of body-text paragraphs, press Alt-Shift-F. This allows you to see more of the outline at once. Pressing Alt-Shift-F again returns full view of the text.

 Select View Draft for the sake of readability. Click Show Icon 2 to display only the two existing heading levels, as shown in Figure 13.1. (The keyboard equivalent is Alt-Shift-2.)

Expanding or Collapsing a Section

You can also show selected levels of just one branch of an outline. The icons to the left of the Show icons on the icon bar, marked plus and minus, expand or collapse a selected section of an outline.

 To select a section, position the mouse pointer on the icon (so that the mouse pointer assumes a plus shape with arrowheads) and click. Select *Plants of the Dunes* in this way, so that this heading and its subheadings are highlighted. Try clicking on the Expand icon in the bar to show body text, and then click on Collapse to hide it again.

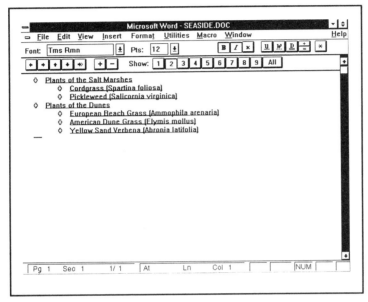

■ *Figure 13.1: Outline view*

Moving a Section

The up arrow and down arrow icons in the icon bar move selected text up and down through the document. Reselect *Plants of the Dunes* to highlight it and its subtext. To transpose this section and the other, click the Move Up (up arrow) icon until *Plants of the Salt Marshes* has shifted below *Yellow Sand Verbena*.

A simpler way to transpose sections is to hide all subtext first. With *Plants of the Dunes* still highlighted, put the major headings back in their original order by clicking Show 1 and then clicking Move Down once.

If you single-click in the selection bar (not on the icon) to the left of a paragraph, you can move that paragraph independently of its currently displayed subtext.

1. Set level 2 again.

2. Move the mouse pointer into the selection bar to the left of *Plants of the Dunes* and click once.

3. Click Move Up—you have effectively classified *pickle-weed* as a dune plant.

4. Click the icon once again to leave *Plants of the Salt Marshes* with no subtext.

5. Click Move Down twice to restore the original order.

Promoting or Demoting a Heading

You can promote and demote any heading from level to level to give it a greater or lesser emphasis within the structure of the document, or as part of reorganizing your text. You can further demote a heading to body text or promote body text to a heading.

Suppose that you wanted to create a new subheading under *Plants of the Dunes* called *Grasses.* This could be the beginning of a new scheme in which each species would be grouped with others of its family common to a given environment.

You can edit in outline view much as you can otherwise. Move the insertion point to the end of the line *Plants of the Dunes,* press Enter, and type **Grasses.** Word for Windows enters the new paragraph as a heading on the same level as the previous one.

The Promote/
Demote icons

1. Select *Grasses* and its new subtext by clicking on its icon.

2. Click the Demote icon (the right arrow that is second from the left end of the icon bar) to demote the heading and its subheadings by one.

3. You now have subheads in the heading-3 style, so click Show 3 to display them.

4. Select *Yellow Sand Verbena* and click Promote (marked with the left arrow, at the far left of the icon bar) to promote it back to level 2.

To reverse this sequence, with heading level 3 showing, highlight *Grasses* by clicking in the selection bar (so that only one line is highlighted), and press Del. Promote the two grasses to level 2 as you did the Yellow Sand Verbena heading.

If the subheads of the deleted heading had also been highlighted, or if they were hidden, they also would have been deleted.

1. Click Show All and then press Alt-Shift-F, if necessary, to display the full text.

2. Move the insertion point to the end of the narrative paragraph for Yellow Sand Verbena and press Enter.

3. Type **Silver Beach Weed (Franseria chamissonis)**—it should appear as body text.

4. Select it by clicking on its icon, and then click on Promote to give it a heading-2 style—it takes on the style of the heading preceding it.

What you just did shows that, instead of applying styles as you did in Step 12, you can type straight text and then promote selected paragraphs to headings.

The Demote To Text icon is the right arrow with the extra point, to the right of the Move Down icon. To see how it works, with the new heading selected, first click Promote to raise it to the heading-1 level, and then click Demote To Text to reduce the heading to body text in one step. Leave it there for a moment.

Demote To Text icon

Shifting Headings with the Mouse

If you find it handy, you can change heading positions and levels with your mouse directly, forgoing the icons. Try these examples:

To promote or demote a paragraph, move the mouse pointer to its icon and drag the icon to the left or right (so that the mouse cursor forms a horizontal double arrow). Continue until an outline box appears in the proper position and a vertical hairline appears that matches the proper indent for the heading level. (To demote a heading to text, drag the icon beyond the rightmost heading level.) For this example, drag the icon for *Silver Beach Weed* to the left to make it a level-2 heading again.

To move a paragraph, move the mouse pointer to the icon and drag the icon up or down (so that the mouse cursor forms a vertical double arrow) until a horizontal hairline appears just where you want to insert the paragraph. For this example, drag the icon for *Silver Beach Weed* upward to insert it before the heading *Yellow Sand Verbena*.

The remainder of this step will show you three simple examples of further possibilities based on outlining. Try them, and then explore variations on your own.

BROWSING WITH YOUR OUTLINE

Using the Split feature of Word for Windows, you can rapidly peruse the text of a long document as you scroll through its headings in outline view.

To split the document window into two panes, use your mouse to drag the Split box (the small oblong at the top of the scroll bar) about halfway down the document window. (You can also make a split by pressing Alt, pressing Enter, selecting Split, positioning the split bar with the Up Arrow and Down Arrow keys, and pressing Enter once again.)

Now, you can switch panes by clicking in a pane or pressing F6. With the insertion point in the lower pane, select View Outline to turn off outline view there. Switch to the upper pane, and, with Show 2 selected, scroll the window by using the scroll bar. Notice that the pane showing the full document scrolls to keep pace, heading by heading. (The effect is more impressive with a longer document.)

Remove the lower pane by dragging the Split box below the document window or by pressing Alt, pressing Enter, selecting Split, positioning the split bar below the document window by pressing Down Arrow, and pressing Enter.

NUMBERING YOUR HEADINGS

A document with graded headings is ideally suited for automatic numbering. Using outline view, you can number sections to any depth that you want. Word for Windows uses one of its field codes to generate section numbers, enabling automatic renumbering as you add, delete, or transpose headings and subtext.

With Show 2 selected, select Utilities Renumber. Highlight *OUT-LINE* and select OK (leave the default options Renumber Paragraphs All and Automatic). Remove the highlighting from the text. Your headings will be numbered in normal outline form. Note that, if you have selected View Field Codes, View Preferences Show All*, or the Star icon in the ribbon, you will see the field codes themselves, not the numbers. Only the displayed levels are numbered.

Try promoting and demoting a few headings with or without their subtext and note how the numbering changes. Now try removing this numbering from your document by selecting Utilities Renumber Remove, and repeat the process using LEGAL Format.

CREATING A TABLE OF CONTENTS

Once you have an outline, it is startlingly easy to generate a table of contents. Try these simple steps:

1. Move the insertion point to the top of the document by pressing Ctrl-Home.

2. Select Insert Table of Contents. Leave the Use Heading Paragraphs and All options selected. Press Enter.

3. Select View Outline to turn off outline view and see the table of contents in its true proportions.

You can now save your work and exit.

Document Review and Revision

Word for Windows is designed to allow readers' systematic review of documents, as well as for controlled incorporation of revisions. In this step, you will learn the following through a few simple examples:

- How you, as author, can prepare a document for review and later read reviewers' annotations

- How you, as a reviewer, can add your annotations to the document

- How you can propose revisions for later review and incorporation into the document

Use the practice document SEASIDE.DOC to try out these examples.

PREPARING FOR REVIEW

As a document's author, you need only pass copies of a document to other Word users (or give them access to it over a network) for them to be able to incorporate annotations. There are, however, some useful options to know about before you pass around the draft document, which include locking the document for annotations and adding comments as hidden text.

Locking a Document

When you lock a document, you prevent anyone but you, its author, from making changes to the text. Users of other copies of Word for Windows with different names (as given in the Utilities Customize dialog box) will be able to add their annotations but will be unable to alter the document's content. This assures that the document returned to you has the same text as when you first circulated it.

To lock the practice text for annotations, simply select File Save As, select the Options command button, and set the Lock for Annotations check box. Follow through by selecting OK.

Adding Hidden Text

Hidden text is any text given the emphasis *hidden* in the Format Character dialog box. It is not included in the printed document or as viewed unless the corresponding view options are selected.

1. Select View Preferences Hidden Text to make hidden text visible.

2. Move the insertion point to the end of the text under *European Beach Grass,* after the phrase "and loss of dune habitat."

3. Type in this sentence:

   ```
   (Should we describe the effects of
   nonnative species? -Author)
   ```

4. Highlight the sentence.

5. Select Forma<u>t</u> <u>C</u>haracter.

6. Set the <u>H</u>idden check box.

Naturally, your reviewers must also make hidden text visible to see your comment. If you want to print hidden text, you can select Options from the File Print menu and set the Include Hidden Text check box.

REVIEWING A DOCUMENT

Put on your reviewer's hat now, and follow these steps:

1. Position the insertion point at the end of the author's note in hidden text.

2. Select <u>I</u>nsert <u>A</u>nnotation. The reviewer's initials, along with the annotation number, appear in brackets after the text, the screen is split into two panes, and the insertion point is positioned after the same bracket notation in the lower pane.

3. Type in this text:

   ```
   Yes, and discuss the effects of the
   explosive spread of ice plant.
   ```

4. Return to the upper pane by clicking in it or pressing F6.

5. Place the insertion point after *Silver Beach Weed (Franseria chamissonis)*.

6. Select <u>I</u>nsert <u>A</u>nnotation.

7. Type

   ```
   Where is the descriptive text?
   ```

By now, your screen should resemble Figure 14.1. Note that a particular reviewer's annotations are numbered in the order of their occurrence in the text. As a reviewer, you could now save the document and exit as usual.

VIEWING ANNOTATIONS

To view annotations, you first select, reasonably enough, View Annotations. (When you first enter an annotation, annotations view is turned on automatically.)

Bring up the first annotation by moving to the beginning of the document, pressing F5 (the Goto key), and entering **a** in response

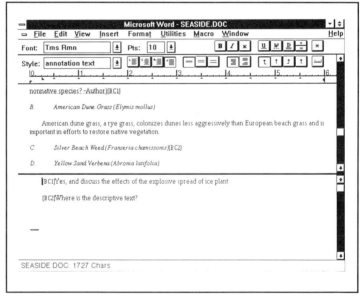

■ *Figure 14.1: The document, with added annotations*

to the *Go to:* prompt in the status bar. You can continue entering **a** to read successive annotations, enter **a** followed by a number (such as **a2**) to jump to that number annotation, or enter, for instance, **a+2** to go forward two annotations or **a-3** to go backward three annotations.

An annotation mark is treated as a single character, so, for instance, you can jump across it by pressing the left or right arrow key once.

Editing
annotations

Try deleting the first annotation: Place the insertion mark to the left of the mark in the text, press Shift-Right Arrow to mark it, and press Del. Both the mark and the annotation text disappear; the second annotation is renumbered automatically.

You can copy, move, or cut and paste an annotation in this way after marking it. You can also move to the annotation window by clicking in it or pressing F6 and can edit the *text* of the annotation by using ordinary methods.

Close the annotation window by dragging the Split box down, or by clicking the menu-bar Control box, selecting Split, and moving the split bar down, so it is off the window.

MARKING REVISIONS

In marking revisions, you record a generation of your edits, not just the results of your edits, in your document. All deleted text is specially marked, and all new text is (or can be) specially marked. If you have not used this form of marking, think of changes to a law in the text of a proposed ballot initiative as an example. Once you have recorded your revisions, Word for Windows enables you to accept and incorporate them all or to reject them.

To begin, select Utilities Revision Marks to bring up the dialog box shown in Figure 14.2, and set the Mark Revisions check box. You can choose whether and where to display a vertical bar to mark revisions, as well as whether and how to mark new text. (Deleted text is always struck through with a horizontal line.) For this example, select Revision Bars Left and Mark New Text With Double Underline. Select OK to begin.

Making a revision

As a quick example, try highlighting *, a rye grass,* under *American Dune Grass,* and type, as a substitution, **is another pioneer that**—note how the old and new text are marked.

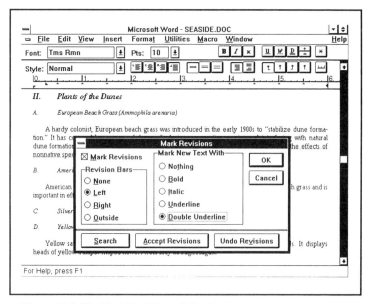

■ *Figure 14.2: The Mark Revisions dialog box*

For a second example, try also deleting the hidden text from the keyboard: Move the insertion point to the beginning of the text. Press Ctrl-Shift-Down Arrow to highlight to the end of the paragraph. Then, press Del.

Select Utilities Revision Marks again, and clear the Mark Revisions check box to end the revision process. Select Accept Revisions, select Yes at the following query (the choices are all or nothing), select OK, and unmark the text to incorporate your revision. (You could also select Undo Revisions and follow a similar sequence to leave the document as it is.) Save the document.

Accepting or undoing revisions

If you save a document under a second file name (using Save As) and then revise the original, Word for Windows will compare the two versions for you. While editing the new document, select Utilities Compare Versions and type the old file name in the Compare File Name text box. The new document will be marked and can be treated as if you had made the changes with Mark Revisions selected, except that, in this case, Word for Windows marks whole paragraphs in which changes have been made.

Adding Documentation

This step shows you how to add some essential features of many documents: headers, footers, footnotes, and endnotes. To begin, bring up your practice document, SEASIDE.DOC.

If your document needs page numbers but no other header or footer matter, you can add them by selecting Insert Page Numbers, selecting a position for the numbers (top or bottom; left, center, or right), and clicking OK.

ADDING HEADERS

Headers and footers are defined for a *section* of a document. To see how this feature can be useful, place a section break in the practice document.

1. Move the insertion point to the end of the last table of contents entry, which should be, *Yellow Sand Verbena* ...1, and select Insert Break.

2. Select the Section Break <u>N</u>ext Page command button to start the second section on a new page, and click OK.

3. Move the insertion point back to any point within the table of contents.

4. If you have page view on, turn it off by selecting <u>V</u>iew <u>P</u>age for a better view of what is to follow.

5. Select <u>E</u>dit <u>H</u>eader/Footer to bring up the corresponding dialog box.

6. Select <u>O</u>ptions for a fuller view of the possibilities, as shown in Figure 15.1.

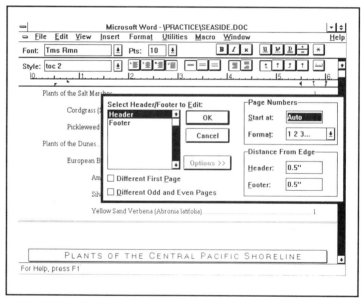

■ *Figure 15.1: The Edit Header/Footer dialog box*

You can set a starting page number by typing it in the Start at: text box; the Auto option starts numbering at 1 or continues it from the previous section. The Format list box allows you to number pages using Roman or Arabic numerals or upper- or lowercase letters. The Distance From Edge text boxes allow you to set spacing from the physical edge of the paper for headers or footers. If you have a laser printer, this spacing must not be closer to the paper edge than the printer can print; if it is, the headers or footers will not appear.

The check boxes in the lower-left corner allow you flexibility in treating the pages of your current document section. Try setting Different First Page, for instance, to see added choices for the first page of the section in the list box. You can edit different contents for first or odd/even page headers and footers within a section, but you can't define separate numbering formats or distances for them. Unset the check box again for now. With Header highlighted for editing, select OK to continue.

Word for Windows opens a *header pane* in the lower part of the screen, with an icon bar. (You will learn about its features in the course of this step). Take a look also at the ruler, which now shows a centered tab stop at midscreen and a right-aligned tab stop at the right margin. These default tab stops make it easy to define up to three elements for a header or footer.

Header pane

Although you can readily type header or footer text, often the information that you need is already provided as fields.

1. Make your document title (available by selecting Edit Summary Info) the first header element by selecting Insert Field, highlighting *Title* in the Insert Field Type list box, and selecting OK. Note that this field has inherited the document's first-line indent. Align it with the left margin by dragging the first-line indent marker in the ruler to 0.

2. Press Tab twice to move to the right-hand tab stop.

3. Select Insert Field again.

4. Highlight *Date.*

5. Highlight the format *MMMM d, yyyy,* and select OK. The date that appears will be updated automatically whenever you print the document.

As shown in Figure 15.2, you have defined a header for your first section, which contains your table of contents.

Linking a header

To adopt the same header for your text, click in the upper pane, move the insertion point to somewhere below the section break, select Edit Header/Footer, and click OK. The icon bar tells you that you are now editing the header for section 2. Select Link to

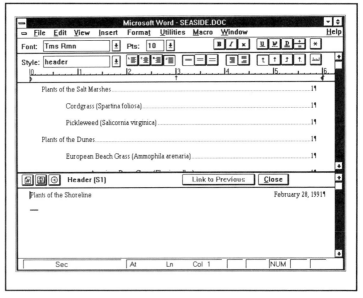

■ *Figure 15.2: The header pane*

Previous and Y̲es at the following prompt to repeat the same header format here.

ADDING FOOTERS

Footers are edited just as headers are. For this example, use footers to display page numbers: Select E̲dit H̲eader/Footer, highlight *Footer,* and select O̲ptions. To start the body of your document text at page 1 instead of numbering from the previous section, type **1** in the S̲tart at: text box. Select OK.

Page numbering options

Reading from the left, the icons allow you quickly to add a page number, date, or time field to a header or footer; however, they offer no flexibility in formatting. You can click on one of them, or press Shift-F10 and then P, D, or T to insert the corresponding field.

Press Tab, type a hyphen, select the page icon, and type another hyphen to add page numbers to footers for your text. Press F6, move the insertion point back into the table of contents, select E̲dit H̲eader/Footer, select O̲ptions and then Page Numbers Forma̲t, highlight the lowercase Roman numerals, and press Enter. Follow the earlier sequence to enter a footer; now, your prefatory matter will be numbered with Roman numerals. Select C̲lose to close the header/footer pane.

ADDING FOOTNOTES AND ENDNOTES

You can easily add footnotes or endnotes to your document, much as you added annotations in the previous step.

Placing Notes

Recall that notes are placed for a whole document as part of document formatting. Select Forma̲t D̲ocument and open the Print A̲t list box to see the possibilities. The choices should be obvious, except for Bottom of Page and Beneath Text. They differ only in that Bottom of Page aligns footnotes against the bottom margin and Beneath Text aligns them up against the text, wherever the page break occurs. Note that you can also set the first note number, or choose to reset numbers at each section break. Click the Cancel button or press Esc to remove the dialog box.

Adding Notes

Move the insertion point to the end of the narrative paragraph for European beach grass, and select Insert Footnote to bring up the dialog box shown in Figure 15.3. You can let your note be numbered in sequence with surrounding notes, or you can type in a

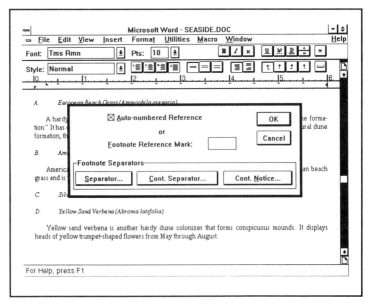

- *Figure 15.3: The Footnote dialog box*

reference mark (the character or characters in the text that refer to the note), in which case a numbering sequence for surrounding notes will bypass this note.

You can also select command buttons to enter new values for the following:

- *Separator:* divides footnotes from the text (normally a 2-inch, horizontal hairline)

- *Continuation Separator:* printed at the bottom margin when a footnote is continued on the following page (normally a hairline running from the left margin to the right margin)

- *Continuation Notice:* text to append to a footnote to announce that it is continued on the following page (no notice is the default value)

Press Enter to accept the default values; the screen splits much the same as it does for annotations, except that the reference mark appears in both panes, and the insertion point is placed in the lower pane. Type in this real reference:

```
California Coastal Commission, California
Coastal Resource Guide (Berkeley: University
of California Press, 1987), p. 19.
```

You can close the footnote pane by selecting View Footnotes. Save the document, and exit Word for Windows.

You can edit, delete, or move notes just as you did annotations in Step 14. You can also find notes by number as you did with annotations. Press F5 and enter f instead of *a* to go to the first or next note.

Including Pictures

■ ■ ■ ■ ■ ■ ■ ■ ■ ■

Pictures are what Lewis Carroll's Alice thought a book was no good without. This is also the Word for Windows term for what you may call *graphics*. You can readily add graphic images from other sources (Windows applications or not) to your Word documents.

Figure 16.1 shows a simple image with caption that has been added to the practice document. This step shows you how to carry out the sequence of steps to incorporate such an image. To begin with, you need an image. The image shown was drawn with Windows Paintbrush and saved in PCX format. Word for Windows was previously installed with the PCX filter to make it possible to read the file.

To begin, bring up the practice document. Select View Page for a realistic view of how elements are placed. Also, set View Preferences Pictures to make pictures visible on-screen.

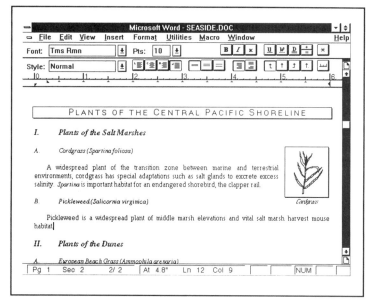

- *Figure 16.1: An added picture*

When you are not actually editing a picture, you can clear View Preferences Pictures to speed redrawing the screen as you browse or edit text.

IMPORTING A PICTURE

Create space for the picture by moving the insertion point to the end of *Plants of the Salt Marshes* and pressing Enter. Select Format Paragraph, set First Line spacing to 0" and Spacing After to *0li,* and select OK. Select Insert Picture, and enter the name of your picture file with its path (if needed) and extension. Word for Windows will insert the picture in your document.

To save yourself the trouble of making a drawing, you can insert a sample image provided with Word for Windows, such as YAWL.TIF in the WINWORD\WINWORD.CBT subdirectory. It will look even less like cordgrass than the picture shown in Figure 16.1, but you can use it to try all the techniques described here. You can also import a picture from another Word for Windows document, or another Windows application, by copying it to the Clipboard and pasting it into place.

If you want a caption, it should appear as a paragraph immediately before or after your picture. Word for Windows treats the picture itself as a paragraph; note that the insertion point to the right of the picture extends to its full height. To insert a caption, press Enter and type **Cordgrass.** Highlight the caption, italicize it by pressing Ctrl-I, and set it for 8 points from the ribbon.

Captions

CROPPING AND SCALING

You can see in the figure that the picture is intended to fit to the right of the next two or three paragraphs. It is helpful to make adjustments to the figure's size before placing it. To this end, Word for Windows allows you to *crop* the picture (trim away its edges) and to *scale* it (change its dimensions). You can do this most quickly and conveniently with a mouse.

Select the picture by clicking within its boundaries. The picture gains a visible outline marked by eight square *sizing handles*. You can use the handles in these ways:

- Drag one of the handles located halfway along each side of the frame to crop the picture along that side.

Using sizing handles

- Drag the handle at a corner to crop the picture along the two adjacent sides.

- Press Shift and then drag a handle to scale the picture. Use a side handle to change its width, use the top or bottom handle to change its height, or use a corner handle to change its overall dimensions in proportion.

As you drag, the status bar shows you the amount of reduction from the picture's original dimensions (as you crop) or the size as a percentage of its original dimensions (as you scale).

Adjust your image to the approximate size of the image shown in the figure, by a combination of cropping and scaling. When you are finished, deselect the figure by clicking elsewhere or moving the insertion point.

 You can crop and scale from the keyboard by selecting Format Picture and entering percents of scale or dimensions to crop as numbers.

POSITIONING A PICTURE

Now that your picture is incorporated in your document, you can position it by ordinary means; for example, to center it, you highlight it and click the Center Paragraph icon in the ruler. If, however, you want to position a picture side by side with text, for instance, you must adopt another technique. Using this technique, you define the picture or other matter as an *absolute object* by assigning it an *absolute position* on the page. Word for Windows can then flow following text around the object.

 Carefully highlight the picture and its caption together by clicking in the picture frame (the outline and boxes will blink) and dragging the mouse pointer to the end of the caption (including the paragraph marker, which you may want to make visible). Release the left mouse button and select Format Position.

To attach the picture and caption to the right margin, highlight Horizontal Position Right and select the Horizontal Relative to Margin command button. Leave the Vertical settings at the default Inline value to allow the picture's position to shift vertically as the surrounding text is edited. You can also leave other settings at their default values, as shown in Figure 16.2. Press Enter.

To finish up, fine-crop and scale the picture to allow the pickle-weed text to run under it. Highlight the caption, and select the Center Paragraph icon to center the text under the picture.

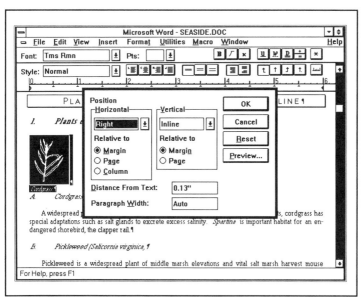

- *Figure 16.2: The Format Position dialog box*

ADDING A BORDER

To add a border, select the picture, select Format Picture, highlight
a border style in the Picture Border text box, and select OK. The
picture shown in the figure uses the Shadow border style.

Save your practice document as always.

Advanced Printing

Word for Windows gives you a number of options covering what part of your document to print and how to print it. In this step, you will learn how to use these options, as well as how to preview the printed appearance of your document. Before moving on to the latter subject, take a moment to recap the subject of document views. As you read about them, try out their effects on the practice document, SEASIDE.DOC.

DOCUMENT VIEWS

All the views that you have used thus far are selected through the View menu:

■ The default view, also called *galley view*, is the approximately full-sized representation of your text that appears when no other view is checked. It offers an accurate display of character and paragraph formatting. With Display As Printed selected under View Preferences, it should also accurately reflect placement of such elements as line and page breaks in your printed copy. With Pictures selected under View Preferences, it will display graphics on-screen, with some loss of speed.

- *Outline view* is the specialized display that you tried in Step 13, which ranks text according to heading levels.

- *Draft view* displays your document in the system font with a minimum of embellishment; it is suited to rapid text entry.

- *Page view* is an extension of galley view that shows all page elements, including headers and footers, notes, multiple columns, and pictures and captions, in their printed positions on each page of your document.

Try selecting page view and scrolling through the practice document to see for yourself how it works. Note that you can jump between pages by clicking on the *page icons* that appear at each end of the vertical scroll bar.

PRINT PREVIEW

Print preview is a reduced representation of a complete page (or of two facing pages) on-screen just as it will be printed. You can do more with print preview, however, than seeing in advance what your output will look like: You can directly manipulate basic page elements to change the layout of a document.

Select File Print Preview to bring up this view of the document. Your options are contained in the icon bar, which also shows the current section (if any) and page numbers. You can switch pages by clicking on the scroll buttons; bring up the second page in this way.

Select Boundaries to reveal the additional markings shown in Figure 17.1. These markings include gray lines marking document margins, each with its small square handle, as well as boxes surrounding the header and footer, the page break, and the picture with its caption (a representative absolute object). You can reposition these elements with the mouse or from the keyboard. When you reposition a margin, the new value takes effect throughout the document.

Raise the bottom margin by positioning the mouse pointer on its handle (so that the pointer becomes cross hairs) and dragging it upward. Move the mouse pointer beyond the left page edge, release the button, and click to complete the action. Move the footer

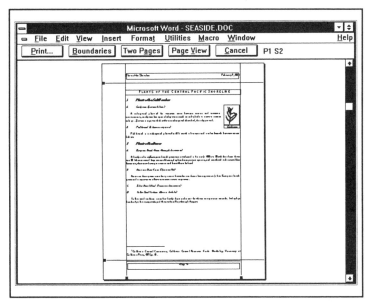

- *Figure 17.1: The Print Preview screen*

higher by positioning the pointer within the box boundaries and
dragging it upward in the same way.

To reposition objects from the keyboard, press Tab until cross
hairs appear at the desired position, move the box or line with the
arrow keys, and press Enter twice.

DECIDING WHAT TO PRINT

Select P̲rint to bring up the Print dialog box that you first encoun-
tered in Step 7 directly from print preview. Select O̲ptions to view
its further possibilities. Open the P̲rint list box, as shown in Figure 17.2, to see your choices for *what* to print: the text of the
document itself, its summary information, reviewers' annotations,

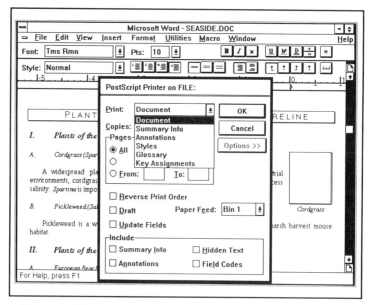

- *Figure 17.2: Print options*

styles, glossary entries (as described in Step 19), or key assignments (standard Word assignments or those that you have defined as macros, also described in Step 19).

The Include check boxes at the bottom of the dialog box select material to be printed *in addition to* the basic Print choice or otherwise modify its appearance. Some or all of these boxes may be unavailable under one choice or another. Included summary information or annotations will be appended to the basic printed text, but hidden text will appear in its place. When you check Field Codes, you choose to print the actual field code itself—for instance, *{title }*—in place of its value, "Plants of the Central Pacific Shoreline."

Recall from Step 7 that precise controls for your printer (such as portrait versus landscape orientation, choice of cartridge font, and resolution) are available under File Printer Setup, Setup.

DECIDING HOW TO PRINT

The Paper Feed list box allows you to choose among paper sources available for your printer—if you choose Manual, Word pauses between pages as you insert paper. If you choose Mixed, Word instructs the printer to feed the first page from Bin 1 and later pages from Bin 2.

The remaining check boxes have these meanings:

- Select Reverse Print Order to have Word send pages to the printer from the last to the first, if this gives you the right collating sequence.

- Select Draft to print rapidly, without character enhancements or pictures.

■ Select Update Fields to update all fields in the document. (Some fields, such as Date, will be updated in any case.)

Try printing the sample document, using one or more of the options described.

Including Tables

■ ■ ■ ■ ■ ■ ■ ■ ■ ■ ■

In this step, you take a whirlwind tour of tables, which offer you simple and flexible means to arrange text and pictures in neat rows and columns and even to perform calculations on ranges of values. There is a lot to this subject, but this lesson gives you a running head start.

CREATING A TABLE FROM NOTHING

For multiple columns between which text can flow freely (known as *snaking* columns), you should use the section-formatting feature described in Step 8. When you want to keep columns of text aligned side by side, however, you need a table.

Tables for columnar text

Open SEASIDE.DOC and then start a new document by selecting File New. Then, select Insert Table. A simple dialog box will prompt you for a number of rows, a number of columns, and an initial column width. You can always start a new table with one row, because rows will appear automatically as you add data.

Although you can add columns, too, without much difficulty, it is good planning to specify the right number from the start.

In this case, accept the default number of 2 columns. You can also accept the initial default column width, Auto. Word for Windows will create two columns of equal width spanning the space between the left and right margins. So, just select OK to create the table.

The two *cells* of the table are surrounded by gray *gridlines* to make them visible—you can control this feature by selecting View Preferences, Table Gridlines. Note that the insertion point is initially placed in the first cell.

Select Windows to switch your active window to SEASIDE.DOC, highlight the heading *A. Cordgrass (Spartina foliosa),* and select Edit Copy. Switch back to the new document, and select Edit Paste. Press Right Arrow to move to the next cell, and repeat this sequence, this time marking the text paragraph under *Cordgrass.*

Note that Word for Windows expands the height of the cell (and other cells in the row) to accommodate the text—it never changes the width, however.

Move the mouse cursor to the left of the text in either cell; you will see a selection bar there. Text in each cell is, in fact, a paragraph, and can be selected or edited as a paragraph. Try moving through either paragraph using the arrow keys—the insertion point will move normally until it reaches a text boundary, when it will jump to the adjoining cell or out of the table. You can also select the text in the next or previous cell by pressing Tab or Shift-Tab, respectively—try it. When you are finished, you can close this document and SEASIDE.DOC without saving changes.

CREATING A TABLE FROM EXISTING TEXT

You can create a table from existing text formed of paragraphs, tabbed material, or comma-delimited records (produced by common databases). For an example using tabs, open your earlier practice document TABSET.DOC.

Highlight the two lines and select <u>I</u>nsert <u>T</u>able. As you can see from Figure 18.1, Word for Windows recognized the tabbed format and counted the existing rows and columns. Press Enter. Note that the left margin plus each tab stop are interpreted as columns.

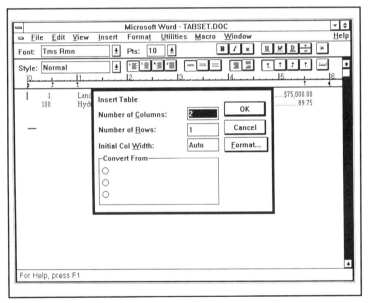

- *Figure 18.1: The Insert Table dialog box*

EDITING A TABLE AS A WHOLE

Try deleting the blank column at the left: Click in the upper-left cell and select Edit Table. The simple dialog box shown in Figure 18.2 gives you two distinct sets of options:

- Select Row or Column to insert or delete an entire row or column of cells at the insertion point.

- Select Selection to insert or delete the cell at the insertion point, to delete a block of cells that you have marked, or to insert new cells next to marked cells. If you are deleting cells and then select Shift Cells Horizontally, cell contents will shift in from the right to fill the void; if you are inserting cells, new cells will appear to the left of the active cell

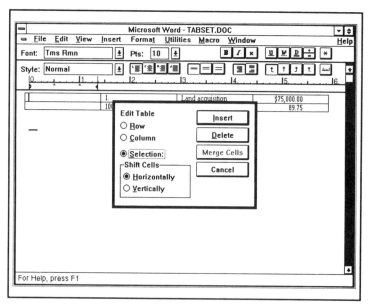

- *Figure 18.2: The Edit Table dialog box*

or marked cell. If you select Shift Cells Vertically, cells will be moved up or down correspondingly.

In this case, select Column and then Delete to remove the empty first column. Bring up the dialog box a second time, and select Row and then Insert to create a heading row.

EDITING CELL CONTENTS

You can edit text in a single cell like any paragraph. You can also select wider blocks of data.

Highlighting Columns or Rows

The easiest way to mark a column is to move the mouse pointer into it and click the right button. Now, move the pointer to the left column, click the right button, and press Del to remove the existing numbers. Replace them with simpler numbering by pressing Down Arrow, typing **1**, pressing Down Arrow, and typing **2**. Mark the column again and click on the Center Paragraph icon in the ruler.

Marking a column

To prepare to mark a row, add a row of column headings:

1. Move the insertion point to the new upper-left cell.

2. Type **Item**.

3. Press Tab and type **Action**.

4. Press Tab and type **Expense**.

You can mark a whole row by moving the mouse pointer to the selection bar for any of its cells and double-clicking. Mark the heading row in this way, and click on the Bold icon in the ribbon and the Center Paragraph icon in the ruler. Select the upper-right cell, and drag the decimal tab stop from the ruler.

Marking a row

You can mark a row or column as described, and copy and paste or cut and paste its contents to a marked destination row or column of the same length.

Appending Data to a Table

It is simple to add data to a table. See for yourself:

1. Move the insertion point to the last row.

2. Press Tab to move it to the last cell.

3. Press Tab once more— a new row appears—and type **3**.

4. Press Tab again and type **Miscellaneous**.

5. Press Tab once more, and type **5.95** to fill the row.

FORMATTING A TABLE

Word for Windows allows you fine control over the proportions and appearance of your table. To adjust the size of a whole table, first mark the whole table. The quickest way to do this is to move the mouse pointer to the leftmost column, press the right mouse button, and drag the mouse pointer across to the rightmost column.

Mark the practice table in this way. Click the ruler view icon to bring up *column view*, in which column boundaries are indicated by T-shaped marks. Drag these marks to reduce the Item and Expense columns to pleasing proportions.

With the table marked, select Format Table to bring up the corresponding dialog box. As shown in Figure 18.3, this box allows you to specify widths for a range of marked columns or for individual columns (if you select the Next Column or Prev Column command buttons), as well as other table dimensions. You can

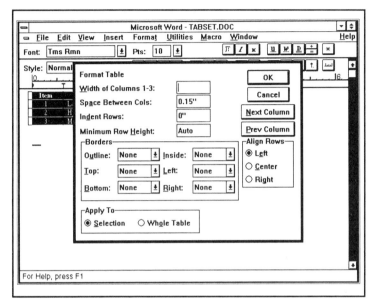

■ *Figure 18.3: The Format Table dialog box*

also use this box to specify a border or inside lines that will print and a row alignment.

Following the figure,

1. Select Outline Double and Inside Single from the Borders list boxes.

2. Select Align Rows Center to center the table between the left and right margins.

3. Leave Width undefined to leave the columns with unequal widths.

4. Select OK and unmark the table.

MAKING CALCULATIONS

To tell you a secret, your table is really an elementary spreadsheet. Try this quick illustration (you can pursue the subject by studying "Tables" and "Fields," subentry "Expression," in your *User's Reference*).

Any table is a coordinate grid in which each cell has an address *rncn*, where you substitute the cell's ordinal row and column number. For instance, looking under *Expense* in your practice table, you can see that the expense for item 1 is *r2c3*, and the expense for item 3 is *r4c3*. The range of addresses that they bound is expressed like this: *[r2c3:r4c3]*. Arithmetical fields can calculate values for ranges like these.

Add a new row to the bottom of your table, and type **Total** as the second column entry. Tab to the third column and select Insert Field. With the = expression highlighted in the Insert Field Type list box, select Field Code and type the following into the text box:

```
=sum([r2c3:r4c3])
```

Don't leave out the equal sign. Then, select Instructions and highlight the format for dollar amounts, which reads

```
$,#,##0.00;($#,##0.00)
```

Don't worry about what this means. Select OK and your total expenses will appear in the selected cell. Save your new table.

Making Model Documents

Sometimes you may need to produce a whole class of documents with various features in common. When this is the case, you should create a *template,* a special kind of document that serves as a prototype for further documents. A template can include *boiler-plate* text for automatic inclusion in all documents based on it, *styles* for paragraph and character formatting, *glossaries*, which are tag names given to blocks of text, and *macros*, which are mouse or keyboard sequences that can be replayed at will. You learned about styles in Step 12; you will be introduced to the other features in this step.

MAKING A TEMPLATE

Start Word for Windows, select File New, and select Template. Press Enter, leaving the Use Template list box set to NORMAL.

The NORMAL template (with the filename NORMAL.DOT) contains the macros, styles, and other settings on which all the documents you create are based. When you create a template, any new

129

settings that you make supersede those in the NORMAL template.

Suppose that you are sending thank-you letters to a few frequent contributors. Enter some boilerplate text (which will include fields and a new feature, *bookmarks*) as the basis for these letters. Open your earlier sample letter COVER.DOC, and copy the inside address:

```
Costabel Wildlife Refuge
Box 1
Costabel, FL 32789
```

1. Mark the paragraph, select the Center Paragraph icon, and set the paragraph to 14-point Helvetica (or the equivalent) from the ribbon.

2. Mark the first line, and select the Small Kaps icon.

3. Move the insertion point to the end of the paragraph, press Enter a few times, and select Insert Field.

4. Highlight Insert Field Type Date, highlight the Instructions format *MMMM d, yyyy,* select Add, and then select OK to add a date field.

5. Highlight the date and assign it 12-point Palatino or a similar font.

Creating a Bookmark

Press Enter a few more times, and click the Left Paragraph icon. Create a bookmark, which is just a named point in the text that you can jump to, to mark where an inside address and salutation will go: Select Insert Bookmark, type the name **address** in the Bookmark Name list box, and press Enter.

Making a Glossary Entry

Suppose that you have a small number of contributors to your organization to whom you frequently send letters. You can store the address for each in a glossary entry.

Go to the first bookmark by pressing F5 and, at the *Go to:* prompt in the status bar, type its name, **address.** Type this address and salutation:

Going to a bookmark

```
Ms. Clare Walker
P.O. Box 100
Point Sur, CA 93100

Dear Ms. Walker:
```

Highlight the address and salutation, and select Edit Glossary. Type in **walker** for the glossary name, select Template for context, and press Enter. This choice of context makes the new entry available only to documents based on this template. Now, delete the highlighted text so that it does not remain as part of the boilerplate itself. You could add more addresses in this fashion.

Press Enter twice and type

```
Thank you for your generous contribution of $
```

Insert another bookmark as you did the first, this time naming it **amount.** Type a period and a space, and go on to say

```
Your continued support has contributed
immeasurably to the success of our project.
You will be happy to hear that American
goldfinches were recently sighted on our
preserve for the first time in twenty years.
```

Press Enter twice, press Tab sufficient times to move the insertion point to the 3" mark, and type **Sincerely yours.** Then, press Enter a few more times, tab over the same distance, and enter a field in a new way: Press Ctrl-F9, type **author** between the braces, and press F9 alone to update the field and put it into effect.

Making a Macro

By defining and using macros, you can automate your most frequent procedures with Word for Windows (such as opening menus and dialog boxes, making selections, marking and copying blocks of text, or setting the ruler) and make them available with a keystroke or menu selection.

In recording a macro, you can incorporate any sequence of keystrokes and mouse movements, except mouse movements to move the insertion point or highlight text—you must perform these actions from the keyboard.

Try recording a simple macro to add *cc:* (the anachronistic "carbon copies") to the end of a letter:

1. Select Macro Record.

2. In the Record Macro Name list box, type in **carbons.**

3. Select Context Template.

4. Select Description and type in a useful description.

5. Select OK.

6. Enter this sequence: Press Ctrl-End, press Enter, press Enter again, type **cc:**, and press Tab.

7. Select Macro Stop Recorder.

8. Delete the added lines and characters.

You can play this macro by selecting <u>M</u>acro <u>R</u>un and highlighting its name in the Run Macro <u>N</u>ame list box (make sure Show <u>A</u>ll is set to show macros in your custom template file), but you can also assign a keystroke or a menu choice to the macro. For practice, try these latter options now.

Select <u>M</u>acro Assign to <u>K</u>ey; from the dialog box (shown in Figure 19.1), select T<u>e</u>mplate in the Context box. Highlight your new macro, *carbons*. You can redefine an existing function-key or Control-key combination. You can also use one of the few undefined Control-key combinations: Press Ctrl-Y, and the choice will appear in the Key box. Press Enter to activate the combination. Press Enter again to return to the editing screen.

Keystroke macros

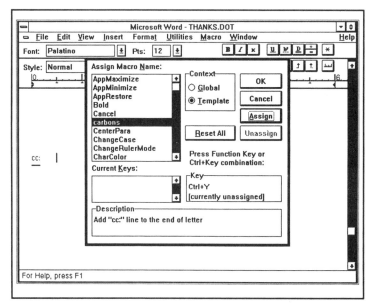

■ *Figure 19.1: The Assign to Key dialog box*

Select Macro Assign to Menu; as before, select Template and highlight your new macro, *carbons*. Note the following:

- The Menu list box contains names from the top-line menu.

- The Menu Text list box contains submenu names for the selected menu.

- The associated text box proposes a name for the new menu item.

- The ampersands represent an underscore for the character following them; that is, they make the following character the selection character.

To make a new entry under Insert, highlight *&Insert* under Menu and select Menu Text. Edit the entry &Carbons to place the ampersand before the letter *r* instead of *C,* since *C* is already a selection letter under Inserts. Press Enter. Verify the new entry from the text screen: Select Insert (note that Carbons now appears as the last item on the menu), and press Esc.

You can edit your macro by selecting Macro Edit. To pursue this topic, print the file TECHREF.DOC in Word's home directory or get a copy of *Word for Windows Technical Reference.*

You are now finished preparing your new template. Select File Save As, and save the template as THANKS.DOT in your practice directory.

USING A TEMPLATE

Now, create a document based on the new template:

1. Select File New and, in the Use Template list box, enter the full path name of your new template. (You need not add the .DOT extension). Select OK.

2. Add the inside address and salutation from the glossary: Go to the first bookmark by pressing F5 and entering **address.** Select Edit Glossary, highlight the entry name *walker,* and select Insert.

3. Press F5, go to the bookmark *amount,* and type in a figure, such as *15.*

4. Run the *carbons* macro by doing one of the following:

    ■   Select Macro Run, highlight the name, and select OK.

    ■   Select Insert Carbons.

    ■   Press Ctrl-Y.

5. Type in any name for a carbon-copy recipient, and save the document.

You can create or edit styles, glossaries, and macros within a document and transfer them to that document's glossary. To do this, after making the changes, just select Format Document and click the Set Default command button.

Designing Form Letters

What you will learn in this step applies to any kind of *merge document*. These simple techniques will save you a lot of labor whenever you must produce regular variations on a basic document.

The practice document for this step is based on the letter template that you created in Step 19. The merge document form will make obvious sense when you have a fairly large database of correspondents.

CREATING A MAIN DOCUMENT

The *main document* contains the boilerplate text in common to all output documents. It also contains special fields (in the Word for Windows sense) that in turn refer to fields (in the database sense) composing a series of records in a file known as the *data document*, which you will create shortly.

Borrow the text for your main document from the template THANKS.DOT: Bring up this file and mark all its contents by moving the mouse pointer to the selection bar, pressing Ctrl, and clicking. Select Edit Copy, File New, OK, and Edit Paste.

Select View Field Codes, go to the address bookmark by pressing F5 and entering **address**, and enter these lines, according to the instructions that follow:

```
{data d:\\practice\\donors.doc}
{ref title} {first} {if{mid} <> "" "{mid} "}{last}
{street}
{city}

Dear {ref title} {last}:
```

Enter the first line as a field by pressing Ctrl-F9, typing the contents, and pressing End to move the insertion point out of the field. The contents include the path name for the data document that you will create. The pairs of backslashes will be interpreted as single backslashes.

Press Enter, press Ctrl-F9, and type **ref title**. *Title* is a *field name* that will designate a field in the donor database. The Word documentation sometimes calls these names "bookmarks," but don't confuse them with bookmarks like those you created in the previous step. *Ref* is a keyword that prevents conflicts between field names and existing field keywords (in the Word for Windows sense). You can add *ref* freely wherever you suspect such a conflict. Press the spacebar and add the *first* field as you did *ref title*. Press the spacebar again.

Use the procedure that follows when a field value may or may not appear in a given record:

1. Press Ctrl-F9, and type **if**.

2. Press Ctrl-F9, and type **mid**.

3. Press Right Arrow, press the spacebar, type <>, press the spacebar, and type " ".

4. Press the spacebar and type ".

5. Press Ctrl-F9, and type **mid**.

6. Press Right Arrow, press the spacebar, and type ".

7. Press End.

This conditional device says, in effect, "If the field 'mid' is not equal to nothing, that is, if there are characters in it, add it." You can use this device to prevent leaving empty spaces or lines in an output document when the corresponding field is empty, as when, for instance, you have provided a company-name field and a given address includes no company name.

Add the remaining fields and text for the address and salutation as you did the *ref title* and *first* fields. Go to the second bookmark, *amount*, press Ctrl-F9, type **gift**, and press End to complete the main document. Save the letter as THANKYOU.DOC.

CREATING A DATA DOCUMENT

The cleanest way to provide merge data is to build a table, much as you did in Step 18. Create a new file, and select Insert Table to insert a table of seven columns and one row. Set the ruler to column mode, and drag the column markers to provide more space for columns 5 and 6 (address and city) and less space for columns 1, 3, and 7 (title, middle initial, and gift). Note, however, that it does no harm if text for a field wraps to a second row within a cell.

Set the font to 12-point Palatino to match your main document and insert the records that follow. Don't press Enter, but, where →

appears in this list, press Tab to move to the next cell:

```
title→first→mid→last→street→city→gift→

Ms→Clare→→Walker→P.O. Box 100→Point Sur, CA
93100→15→

Rev→Arthur→A.→Barclay→10 Malpaso Creek
Rd→Point Pinos, CA 93101→50

Mr→Lee→→Cawdor→Cawdor Ranch→Bixby's
Landing, CA 93100→9.95
```

As you see, the first record in the table provides the field names. Save this document as DONORS.DOC in your practice directory.

 Rather than formatting characters in the data document to match those in the main document, you can format the field names in the main document to print as you like and add the switch *charformat to the field, like this:

```
{first\*charformat}
```

This will allow you to use the same field names in different formats at different points in the same main document.

 As an alternative to the table form, you can set up your data document in the form of records with fields separated by commas or other characters. See your *User's Reference* for treatment of special characters (commas, double quotation marks, and certain other characters) in these records and for more information on merge documents; refer to the headings "Merging Documents," "Form Letters," and "Address Labels."

PRINTING A MERGE DOCUMENT

To print your final documents, select File Print Merge and make the simple choices in the dialog box shown in Figure 20.1:

- Leave the All option selected to print all records, or select From, enter a record number, select To, and enter a record number.

- Select Print to print each selected document, or select New Document. In the latter case, the new document will appear in a window, with each merged record appearing on a page of its own. You can edit, print, and save this document like any other.

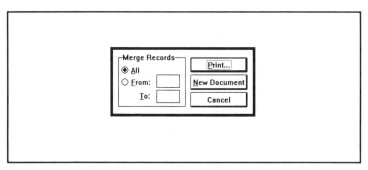

- *Figure 20.1: The Print Merge dialog box*

■ ■ ■ ■ ■ ■ ■ ■

Format Paragraph dialog box, 59–65
Format Picture command, 114
Format Position dialog box, 113
Format Section dialog box, 55–57
Format Styles command, 82
Format Table dialog box, 126–127
Format Tabs command, 64
formatting
  alternatives for, 83
  of characters, 67–72
  copying, 65
  of documents, 52–54
  keystrokes for, 69–70
  of paragraphs, 59–65
  with ribbon, 74–75
  with ruler, 75–77
  searching for, 36
  of sections, 55–57
  with styles, 79–83
  of tables, 126–127
full menu mode, 10

G

galley view, 115
glossary entries, 131–132
graphics. *See* pictures
graphics filters, installing, 3
gridlines, 122
gutter margin, 52

H

handles, 111–112
hanging indentation, 60
headers, 101–105
headings, outline, 80–81, 86
  numbering, 91–92
  promoting/demoting, 88–90
help system, 14–15
hidden text, 94–95
hyphenation, 70–72

I

indentation, 59–60, 76
Ins key, 22
Insert Annotation command, 95
Insert Bookmark command, 130
Insert Break command, 55
Insert Field command, 21, 103–104, 128
Insert Footnote command, 106–107
Insert mode, 22
Insert Page Numbers command, 101
Insert Picture command, 110
Insert Table command, 123, 139
insertion point, 7, 14
installing Word for Windows, 1–4
italic text, 69–70, 75

J

joining paragraphs, 23, 65
jump terms, 14
justifying text, 61, 76

K

keyboard
  applying character formatting with, 69–70
  moving insertion point with, 13, 23
  scaling pictures with, 112
  selecting dialog box features with, 12
  selecting menu options with, 9–10
  selecting text with, 28
keyboard template, 13

L

laser printers, setup for, 46–47
leaders, tab, 63–64
left-aligned text, 61, 76
left-indent marker, 59–60, 76

letters, form, 137–141
line breaks, 70–72
line numbering, 56, 65
line spacing, 61–62, 76
loading Word for Windows, 7
long documents, 90–91
lowercase characters, 35

M

macros, 132–134
mail merge. *See* merging files
main documents, 137–139
manual hyphenation, 70–72
margin view, 75
margins, 52–53
  changing, 54, 75
  mirror, 53, 54
  repositioning in Print Preview,
    117–118
Mark Revisions dialog box, 98–99
mathematical expressions, 128
Maximize box, 9
memory requirements, 1–2
menu bar, 9–10
menus, 9–10
  adding macros to, 134
  long vs. short, 10
merging files, 141
Microsoft Windows, 1
  adding Word to, 4
  Print Manager, 47–49
  running Setup program from, 2
Microsoft Word. *See* Word for Windows
Minimize box, 9
mirror margins, 53, 54
mouse
  cropping pictures with, 111–112
  moving insertion point with, 14, 22
  scrolling with, 14, 90–91
  selecting dialog box features with,
    11–12
  selecting menu options with, 9

selecting text with, 26–28
shifting outline headings with, 90
mouse pointer, 14
moving text, 31
multiple columns, 55, 121–122

N

naming documents, 23
new file dialog box, 17–18
newlines, 21
newspaper-style columns, 55, 121
Normal style, 80
NORMAL.DOT file, 17, 129
numbering
  footnotes, 106–107
  lines, 56, 65
  pages, 101, 103, 105

O

opening documents, 25–26
option buttons, 11–12
orphans, 54
outline view, 85–87, 116
outlining, 85–92
overtype mode, 22
OVR indicator, 22

P

page breaks, 65
page height, 52, 53
page numbers
  automatic, 103
  in footers, 105
  in sections, 103
  simple, 101
page size, 53
page view, 116
page width, 52, 53
panes, 14
  for browsing outlines, 90–91

scrolling in, 90–91
  for viewing annotations, 95–97
  for viewing footnotes, 107
paper feed, 119
paper sizes, 53
paragraph marks
  copying, 65
  deleting, 65
  hiding, 32
  viewing, 21, 22
paragraph view, 75–76
paragraphs, 20–21
  aligning, 56–57, 61–62
  boxing, 61
  copying formatting of, 65
  formatting, 59–65
  indenting, 59–60
  joining, 23, 65
  justified, 61
  keeping together, 64–65
  reformatting, 65
  spacing between, 62
  splitting, 22–23
Paste command, 31
pasting. *See* cutting and pasting
PCX files, 3, 109
PIC files, 3
pictures
  cropping, 111–112
  importing, 110–111
  positioning, 112–113
  scaling, 111–112
point size, 12, 68, 74
previewing documents, 116–118
Print dialog box, 47, 48, 118–120
Print Manager (Windows), 47–49
Print Merge command, 141
Print Preview command, 116–118
print queue, 47–49
printer drivers, 3
printers
  setting up, 45–47
  unsupported, 3
printing

of annotations, 118, 119
of document summaries, 118, 119
of documents, 47, 118–120
in draft mode, 119
of field codes, 119
of form letters, 141
of glossary entries, 119
of hidden text, 119
of key assignments, 119
in landscape mode, 47
merged, 141
of multiple copies, 47
in portrait mode, 47
queued, 47–49
in reverse page order, 119
of selected pages, 47
Program Manager (Windows), 2, 4, 5, 7,
    45, 49
program window, 8–9

Q

question mark (?) as wildcard character,
    35
queued printing, 47–49
quitting Word for Windows, 15
quotation marks, 72

R

records, 140
repeating searches, 34, 35
replacing text, 30, 36–37
reviewing documents, 95–96
revisions, marking, 97–99
ribbon, 12
  formatting with, 74–75
  removing, 12
  viewing, 73
right-aligned text, 61, 76
right-indent marker, 59–60, 76
ruler, 12–13
  aligning text with, 76

removing, 13
setting line spacing with, 76
setting margins with, 75
setting tab stops with, 76–77
viewing, 73
ruler-view icon, 75, 126

S

Save command, 31–32
Save As command, 23
saving documents, 23, 31–32
screen display, 8–9
scroll bar, 14
scroll box, 14
scroll buttons, 14
scrolling, 14, 90–91
Search dialog box, 33–35
searching
  for formats, 36
  repeat key for, 34, 35
  for special characters, 35
  for text, 33–35
sections, 51, 55–57
selecting text, 25, 26–30
selection bar, 22, 27–28
Setup program, 2–3
Shift-Del (Cut), 31
Shift-Enter, 20
Shift-Ins (Paste), 31
short menu mode, 10
single spacing, 61, 76
sizing handles, 111–112
small capitals, 69
space characters, 72
spacing
  of characters, 69
  of lines, 61–62, 76
  between paragraphs, 62
special characters
  adding, 72
  searching for, 35
spelling checker, 39–42

Spelling dialog box, 41–42
Split box, 14. *See also* panes
splitting paragraphs, 22–23
starting Word for Windows, 7
status bar, 13
style area, 83
styles, 79–83
summary information dialog box,
  18–20

T

tab leaders, 63–64
tab stops
  centered, 77
  changing, 76–77
  custom, 62–64, 77
  decimal, 64, 77
  default, 53–54
  deleting, 64, 77
  editing from ruler, 76–77
  left-aligned, 77
  navigating, 64
  right-aligned, 77
  setting from Format Tabs dialog box,
    62–64
tables
  adding lines to, 126
  calculations in, 128
  creating, 121–123
  editing, 124–125
  editing text in, 125–126
  formatting, 126–127
Tabs dialog box, 63, 64, 81
templates, 17, 129–135
text
  aligning, 56–57, 61–62, 76
  boldface, 68, 69, 82–83
  boxing, 61
  centering, 61, 76
  color of, 69
  copying, 31
  cutting and pasting, 30–31